CIVICS 105

DOCUMENTS THAT FORMED AMERICA

ROGER L. KEMP

authorHOUSE

AuthorHouse™
1663 Liberty Drive
Bloomington, IN 47403
www.authorhouse.com
Phone: 833-262-8899

Published by AuthorHouse 08/17/2021

ISBN: 978-1-6655-3523-6 (sc)
ISBN: 978-1-6655-3522-9 (e)

Library of Congress Control Number: 2021916926

DEDICATION

This book is dedicated to Kieran,
The best and the brightest

ACKNOWLEDGEMENTS

Grateful acknowledgements are made to the elected officials, appointed officials, and citizens, of those cities that I have worked and lived in during my over a quarter-century public service career on both coasts of the United States.

These states and cities include the following:

- In California   –   The City of Oakland
  The City of Seaside
  The City of Placentia
  The City of Vallejo

- In New Jersey   –   The City of Clifton

- In Connecticut   –   The City of Meriden
  The Town of Berlin

CONTENTS

Lesson9: The Constitution of the United States

Lesson10: The Bill of Rights

Lesson11: Other Amendments to the Constitution of the United States

Lesson12: The Civil Rights Act

Lesson13: The Voting Rights Act

The Future

PREFACE

American citizens have a lot to be proud of! They live in one of the oldest democratic forms of government in the world, and this form of government has helped create a society in which citizens are free to get involved in the political process. Citizens can vote, run for political office, endorse incumbents, promote new public office seekers, or merely back other people who do so. Also, between elections citizens are free to attend public meetings, many of which are required by law, speak about their policy and program preferences at these meetings, write letters to the editor, and even organize others to get involved in "their" political agenda.

The involvement of citizens in the American political process has changed over the years. For many years, citizens believed in *Jacksonian Democracy*, whereby they would get directly involved in the political process by attending meetings, advocating for pieces of legislation, or trying to change or invalidate legislation that they did not like. This political activism on the part of citizens primarily took place before the era of two income families, before there came to be little time for this type of political involvement. Democracy in America was founded on the principle of active political involvement on the part of its citizens.

Most adult households now have both parents working, and family time is limited to a few hours in the evenings after work. Many citizens nowadays merely elect their political representatives, and hold them accountable at voting time from election to election. This evolving type of democratic involvement on the part of citizens is called *Jeffersonian Democracy*. Many citizens have justified this type of political involvement by acknowledging that elections and voting give the common person a chance to elect the uncommon person to represent them. Under this evolving practice, the typical involvement of many citizens in the political process is merely voting at election time.

The political involvement of many Americans in years past included picketing, protesting, marching, signing petitions, attending public meetings, and publicly debating the issues. Today Americans may wear a political button, display a bumper sticker on their car, or place a candidate's sign in their front yard. Many citizens may also contribute financially to political campaigns. Because of other social and economic commitments, American citizens have evolved throughout history from engaging in very active political involvement to more passive political activities.

Everyone will agree that there is no perfect form of government, and the best form is one that has evolved and changed over time to best serve its citizens. Most citizens today take their form of government for granted. After all, it is the only form of government they have ever known. While history is provided to students in high school and college, little time is spent focusing on how our country's democratic form of government was established and, most importantly, how it has evolved over time to become one of the most respected national governments in the world. Many history classes start with the landing of the Pilgrims, and never cover the background and mind-set of the early settlers from the Kingdom of England. They had a form of government that greatly influenced and impacted the early settlers in the New World.

This volume focuses on the basics of the formation of America's democracy, and the changes that have taken place over the years through legislation, constitutional amendments, supreme court decisions, and the impact of the evolution of our culture over time on our political processes. Many of the political changes to our democracy, and its form of government, resulted over time in response to changing citizen values and expectations. As American society evolved, so did many aspects of its democracy. These changes have manifested themselves in every changing political process, new and revised laws and regulations, as well as the magnitude and type of services provided by its governments.

For ease of reference, this volume is divided into eleven sections. These sections introduce the reader to the subject of American democracy. Section three, this book contains the core documents that established our democratic form of government. The final section examines the future of democracy, as well as its worldwide implications. Several appendices are also included to provide the reader with a greater understanding of the complex and dynamic field of America's democracy.

The Core Documents

Various documents helped form America's democratic form of government, starting with those created by the Pilgrims soon after their landing in an unfamiliar part of the world far from their home. The original colonists were loyal to England, and it took a war to emancipate the colonies and their residents, the colonists, from the government of their homeland. During this time colonies emerged, citizens were elected to hold public office, wars were fought, treaties were negotiated, and even amendments were made to the basic documents of government over the years. The documents examined in this section include:

- The *Mayflower Compact*, which was signed by the Pilgrims of the New World on November 21, 1620. The first document in the New World was signed to preserve order and establish rules for self-governance.
- The *Fundamental Orders of Connecticut*, which were approved by the Colony Council on January 14, 1639. This document is considered the first written constitution establishing a formal government in the New World.
- The *Declaration and Resolves of the First Continental Congress*, which were approved by the Continental Congress on October 14, 1774. This document was created to make the King and Parliament of England officially aware of the grievances of the colonies.
- The *Declaration of the Causes and Necessity of Taking Up Arms*, which was approved by the Continental Congress on July 6, 1775. This document was prepared to explain why the Thirteen Colonies had taken up arms against England in a battle that was later called the American Revolution.
- The *Virginia Declaration of Rights*, which was approved by the House of Burgesses on June 12, 1776. This document reflects the first declaration of the rights of citizens by a colony in the New World.

- The *Declaration of Independence*, which was approved by the Continental Congress on July 4, 1776. This document is the product of the early days of the Revolutionary War, and officially declared the independence of the American colonies from Great Britain.
- The *Constitution of Massachusetts*, which was approved by the State Constitutional Convention Representatives on June 15, 1780. This document is the oldest functioning written constitution in continuous use by any government in the world.
- The *Articles of Confederation*, which were approved by the Congress of the Confederation on March 1, 1781. This document is historically recognized as the first constitution of the United States of America.
- The *Constitution of the United States*, which was approved by the Congress of the Confederation on September 17, 1787. The original constitution is known as the supreme law of the United States. It provides the foundation, and source of legal authority, as well as built-in checks-and-balances, for the United States and its federal government.
- The *Bill of Rights*, which was approved by the United States Congress on December 15, 1791. This document reflects the first ten amendments to the United States Constitution. While introduced by James Madison in the First United States Congress in 1789, they were not effective until approved by three-fourths of the states two years later.
- The *Other Amendments to the Constitution of the United States*, which were approved by the United States Congress between February 7, 1795 and May 7, 1992. The Constitution of the United States contains an amendment process. This document includes those amendments made to the Constitution since the passage of the Bill.

The Future

The final chapter of this volume, *The Future of Democracy*, examines the impact that democracy has had on the United States of America, as well as the goal of its government to advance freedom and democracy throughout the world over the years. The author discusses the history of America's democracy, including past problems and threats, and goes on to examine international threats facing our nation and its citizens, as well as their form of government. The author states that the underlying theme of American history has been the willingness of our government, as influenced by its politicians, to defend our security and our interests in ways that, in the long run, have led to the expansion of democratic values and institutions. He concludes by stating that America, and its form of government, is looked upon as a model to emulate by citizens of other countries throughout the world.

Appendices

Many hours were spent researching the valuable resource materials contained in this volume. Since this volume focuses on documents, every effort was made to provide background information for the reader to become more familiar with the history of America's democratic form of governance, and the various documents that created it.

Lastly, the appendices at the end of this volume include a glossary of government terms, a history of citizen voting rights in our nation, as well as state and natural government resource directories. Closing appendices include a listing of books by the author, the world travel during his public service career, and some important information.

Roger L. Kemp

LESSON ONE

THE MAYFLOWER COMPACT

Mayflower Compact

(November 21, 1620)

Pilgrims of the New World

▐ The History[1]*

The settlers who came to the New World brought with them a great deal of baggage in the form of ideas and beliefs they had held dear in England. Indeed, many of them, such as the Puritans, came to America so they could live in stricter accord with those beliefs. The Pilgrims, a branch of the Puritans, arrived off the coast of Massachusetts in November 1620, determined to live sacred lives according to biblical commands, and in so doing to build a "city upon a hill" that would be a beacon to the rest of the world.

But aside from their religious enthusiasm, the Pilgrims also knew that the English settlement founded a few years earlier at Jamestown in Virginia had practically foundered because of the lack of a strong government and leadership. They would not make that mistake, and agreed that once a government had been established, they would obey the commands of its leaders.

In making this compact, the Pilgrims drew upon two strong traditions. One was the notion of a social contract, which dated back to biblical times and which would receive fuller expression in the works of Thomas Hobbes and John Locke later in the century. The other was the belief in covenants. Puritans believed that covenants existed not only between God and man, but also between man and man. The Pilgrims had used covenants in establishing their congregations in the Old World. The Mayflower Compact is such a covenant in that the settlers agreed to form a government and be bound by its rules.

The Compact is often described as America's first constitution, but it is not a constitution in the sense of being a fundamental framework of government. Its importance lies in the belief that government is a form of covenant, and that for government to be legitimate, it must derive from the consent of the governed. The settlers recognized that individually they might not agree with all of the actions of the government they were creating; but they, and succeeding generations, understood that government could be legitimate only if it originated with the consent of those it claimed to govern.

On November 21, 1620, forty-one adult male passengers signed the Mayflower Compact. The compact served as a device to preserve order and establish rules for self-government. The signers agreed to combine themselves into a "civil Body Politick" that would enact and obey "just and

---

[1] * Originally published as "The Mayflower Compact (1620)," *Basic Readings in U.S. Democracy*, InfoUSA, Bureau of International Information Programs, U.S. Department of State, Washington, DC, 2009. For additional information see "Pilgrims," *Cape Cod National Seashore History and Culture*, National Park Service, U.S. Department of the Interior, Washington, DC, 2007. This agency is listed in the *National Resource Directory* section of this volume.

equal laws" that were made for the "general good of the colony." This commitment to justice and equality would be reiterated in many later documents, including the U.S. Constitution.

There were two other colonies in the New World prior to the landing of the Pilgrims in 1620. The first was the Roanoke Colony, which was located on Roanoke Island in the Virginia Colony and financed by Sir Walter Raleigh in the late 16th century. Between 1585 and 1587, several groups attempted to establish this colony, but had abandoned the settlement. The final group of colonists disappeared after three years had elapsed without receiving supplies from the Kingdom of England during the Anglo-Spanish War, leading to the continuing mystery commonly known as "The Lost Colony."

The second settlement was the first successful English settlement in the New World. Named after King James I of England, Jamestown was founded in the Virginia Colony in May of 1607. Jamestown was founded for the purpose of making a profit from gold mining for its investors, while also establishing a permanent foothold in the New World for England. These settlers were given a charter and funded by the Virginia Company, a private corporation. Other successful colonies in North America were in Spanish dominions such as New Spain, New Mexico, and Spanish Florida.

Because the first settlement at Roanoke did not materialize, and the second settlement at Jamestown was a private venture, the Pilgrims are recognized as the first group of emigrants to the New World to draft their own charter, or compact as they called it, and to establish their own civil society with a governmental structure.

▌The Document

Mayflower Compact

We whose names are underwritten, the loyal subjects of our dread Sovereign Lord King James, by the Grace of God of Great Britain, France and Ireland, King, Defender of the Faith, etc.

Having undertaken, for the Glory of God and advancement of the Christian Faith and Honour of our King and Country, a Voyage to plant the First Colony in the Northern Parts of Virginia, do by these presents solemnly and mutually in the presence of God and one of another, Covenant and Combine ourselves together into a Civil Body Politic, for our better ordering and preservation and furtherance of the end aforesaid; and by virtue hereof to enact, constitute and frame such just and equal Laws, Ordinances, Acts, Constitutions and Offices, from time to time, as shall be thought most meet and convenient for the general good of the Colony, unto which we promise all due submission and obedience. In witness whereof we have hereunder subscribed our names at Cape Cod, the 11th of November, in the year of the reign of our Sovereign Lord King James, of England, France and Ireland the eighteenth, and of Scotland the fifty-fourth. Anno Domini 1620.

– Signed by forty-one (41) adult male passengers.

LESSON TWO

THE FUNDAMENTAL ORDERS OF CONNECTICUT

Fundamental Orders of Connecticut

(January 14, 1639)

Colony Council

The History[2]*

The Fundamental Orders were adopted by the Connecticut Colony council on January 14, 1639.[1] [2] The orders describe the government set up by the Connecticut River towns, setting its structure and powers.

It has the features of a written constitution, and is considered by some as the first written Constitution in the Western tradition,[3] and thus earned Connecticut its nickname of *The Constitution State*. John Fiske, a Connecticut historian, was the first to claim that the Fundamental Orders were the first written Constitution, a claim disputed by some modern historians.[4] The orders were transcribed into the official colony records by the colony's secretary Thomas Welles. It was a Constitution for the colonial government of Hartford and was similar to the government Massachusetts had set up. However, this Order gave men more voting rights and opened up more men to be able to run for office positions.

In 1635 a group of Massachusetts Puritans and Congregationalists who were dissatisfied with the rate of Anglican reforms, sought to establish an ecclesiastical society subject to their own rules and regulations. The Massachusetts General Court granted them permission to settle the cities of Springfield, Windsor, Wethersfield, and Hartford.[5] Ownership of the land was called into dispute by the English holders of the Warwick Patent of 1631. The Massachusetts General Court established the March Commission to mediate the dispute, and named Roger Ludlow as its head. The Commission named 8 magistrates from the Connecticut towns to implement a legal system. The March commission expired in March 1636, after which time the settlers continued to self-govern. On May 29, 1638 Ludlow wrote to Massachusetts Governor Winthrop that the colonists wanted to "unite ourselves to walk and lie peaceably and lovingly together." Ludlow drafted the Fundamental Orders, which were adopted on January 14, 1639, which established Connecticut as a self-ruled entity.

There is no record of the debates or proceedings of the drafting or enactment of the Fundamental Orders. It is postulated that the farmers wished to remain anonymous to avoid retaliation by the English authorities. According to John Taylor:[6]

---

2 * Originally published as "Fundamental Orders of Connecticut," *Wikipedia*, Wikimedia Foundation, Inc., San Francisco, California, December 2008. For additional information see "The First Constitution of Connecticut," *Historical Antecedents*, Secretary of State, State of Connecticut, Hartford, Connecticut, 2008. This agency is listed in the *National Resource Directory* section of this volume.

The men of the three towns were a law unto themselves. It is known that they were in earnest for the establishment of a government on broad lines; and it is certain that the ministers and captains, the magistrates and men of affairs, forceful in the settlements from the beginning, were the men who took the lead, guided the discussions, and found the root of the whole matter in the first written declaration of independence in these historical orders.

The Fundamental Orders of Connecticut is a short document, but it contains some principles that were later applied in creating the United States government. Government is based in the rights of an individual, and the orders spell out some of those rights, as well as how they are ensured by the government. It provides that all free men share in electing their magistrates, and uses secret, paper ballots. It states the powers of the government, and some limits within which that power is exercised.

In one sense, the Fundamental Orders were replaced by a Royal Charter in 1662, but the major outline of the charter was written in Connecticut and embodied the Orders' rights and mechanics. It was carried to England by Governor John Winthrop and basically approved by the British King, Charles II. The colonists generally viewed the charter as a continuation and surety for their Fundamental Orders; the Charter Oak got its name when that charter was supposedly hidden in it, rather than be surrendered to the King's agents.

Today, the individual rights in the Orders, with others added over the years, are still included as a "Declaration of Rights" in the first article of the current Connecticut Constitution, adopted in 1965.

▌ The Document

Fundamental Orders

For as much as it hath pleased Almighty God by the wise disposition of his divine providence so to order and dispose of things that we the Inhabitants and Residents of Windsor, Hartford and Wethersfield are now cohabiting and dwelling in and upon the River of Connectecotte and the lands thereunto adjoining; and well knowing where a people are gathered together the word of God requires that to maintain the peace and union of such a people there should be an orderly and decent Government established according to God, to order and dispose of the affairs of the people at all seasons as occasion shall require; do therefore associate and conjoin ourselves to be as one Public State or Commonwealth; and do for ourselves and our successors and such as shall be adjoined to us at any time hereafter, enter into Combination and Confederation together, to maintain and preserve the liberty and purity of the Gospel of our Lord Jesus which we now profess, as also, the discipline of the Churches, which according to the truth of the said Gospel is now practiced amongst us; as also in our civil affairs to be guided and governed according to such Laws, Rules, Orders and Decrees as shall be made, ordered, and decreed as followeth:

1. It is Ordered, sentenced, and decreed, that there shall be yearly two General Assemblies or Courts, the one the second Thursday in April, the other the second Thursday in September following; the first shall be called the Court of Election, wherein shall be yearly chosen from time to time, so many Magistrates and other public Officers as shall be found requisite: Whereof one to be chosen Governor for the year ensuing and until another be chosen, and no other Magistrate to be chosen for more than one year: provided always there be six chosen besides the Governor, which being chosen and sworn according to an Oath recorded for that purpose, shall have the power to administer justice according to the Laws here established, and for want thereof, according to the Rule of the Word of God; which choice shall be made by all that are admitted freemen and have taken the Oath of Fidelity, and do cohabit within this Jurisdiction having been admitted Inhabitants by the major part of the Town wherein they live or the major part of such as shall be then present.

2. It is Ordered, sentenced, and decreed, that the election of the aforesaid Magistrates shall be in this manner: every person present and qualified for choice shall bring in (to the person deputed to receive them) one single paper with the name of him written in it whom he desires to have Governor, and that he that hath the greatest number of papers shall be Governor for that year. And the rest of the Magistrates or public officers to be chosen in this manner: the Secretary for the time being shall first read the names of all that are to be put to choice and then shall severally nominate them distinctly, and every one that would have the person nominated to be chosen shall bring in one single paper written upon, and he that would not have him chosen shall bring in a blank; and every one that hath more written papers than blanks shall be a Magistrate for that year; which papers shall be received and told by one or more that shall be then chosen by the court and sworn to be faithful therein; but in case there should not be six chosen as aforesaid, besides the Governor, out of those which are nominated, then he or they which have the most writen papers shall be a Magistrate or Magistrates for the ensuing year, to make up the aforesaid number.

3. It is Ordered, sentenced, and decreed, that the Secretary shall not nominate any person, nor shall any person be chosen newly into the Magistracy which was not propounded in some General Court before, to be nominated the next election; and to that end it shall be lawful for each of the Towns aforesaid by their deputies to nominate any two whom they conceive fit to be put to election; and the Court may add so many more as they judge requisite.

4. It is Ordered, sentenced, and decreed, that no person be chosen Governor above once in two years, and that the Governor be always a member of some approved Congregation, and formerly of the Magistracy within this Jurisdiction; and that all the Magistrates, Freemen of this Commonwealth; and that no Magistrate or other public officer shall execute any part of his or their office before they are severally sworn, which shall be done in the face of the court if they be present, and in case of absence by some deputed for that purpose.

5. It is Ordered, sentenced, and decreed, that to the aforesaid Court of Election the several Towns shall send their deputies, and when the Elections are ended they may proceed in any public service as at other Courts. Also the other General Court in September shall be for making of laws, and any other public occasion, which concerns the good of the Commonwealth.

6. It is Ordered, sentenced, and decreed, that the Governor shall, either by himself or by the

Secretary, send out summons to the Constables of every Town for the calling of these two standing Courts one month at least before their several times: And also if the Governor and the greatest part of the Magistrates see cause upon any special occasion to call a General Court, they may give order to the Secretary so to do within fourteen days' warning: And if urgent necessity so required, upon a shorter notice, giving sufficient grounds for it to the deputies when they meet, or else be questioned for the same. And if the Governor and major part of Magistrates shall either neglect or refuse to call the two General standing Courts or either of them, as also at other times when the occasions of the Commonwealth require, the Freemen thereof, or the major part of them, shall petition to them so to do; if then it be either denied or neglected, the said Freemen, or the major part of them, shall have the power to give order to the Constables of the several Towns to do the same, and so may meet together, and choose to themselves a Moderator, and may proceed to do any act of power which any other General Courts may.

7. It is Ordered, sentenced, and decreed, that after there are warrants given out for any of the said General Courts, the Constable or Constables of each Town, shall forthwith give notice distinctly to the inhabitants of the same, in some public assembly or by going or sending from house to house, that at a place and time by him or them limited and set, they meet and assemble themselves together to elect and choose certain deputies to be at the General Court then following to agitate the affairs of the Commonwealth; which said deputies shall be chosen by all that are admitted Inhabitants in the several Towns and have taken the oath of fidelity; provided that none be chosen a Deputy for any General Court which is not a Freeman of this Commonwealth.

The aforesaid deputies shall be chosen in manner following: every person that is present and qualified as before expressed, shall bring the names of such, written in several papers, as they desire to have chosen for that employment, and these three or four, more or less, being the number agreed on to be chosen for that time, that have the greatest number of papers written for them shall be deputies for that Court; whose names shall be endorsed on the back side of the warrant and returned into the Court, with the Constable or Constables' hand unto the same.

8. It is Ordered, sentenced, and decreed, that Windsor, Hartford, and Wethersfield shall have power, each Town, to send four of their Freemen as their deputies to every General Court; and Whatsoever other Town shall be hereafter added to this Jurisdiction, they shall send so many deputies as the Court shall judge meet, a reasonable proportion to the number of Freemen that are in the said Towns being to be attended therein; which deputies shall have the power of the whole Town to give their votes and allowance to all such laws and orders as may be for the public good, and unto which the said Towns are to be bound.

9. It is Ordered, sentenced, and decreed, that the deputies thus chosen shall have power and liberty to appoint a time and a place of meeting together before any General Court, to advise and consult of all such things as may concern the good of the public, as also to examine their own Elections, whether according to the order, and if they or the greatest part of them find any election to be illegal they may seclude such for present from their meeting, and return the same and their reasons to the Court; and if it be proved true, the Court may fine the party or parties so intruding, and the Town, if they see cause, and give out a warrant to go to a new election in a legal way, either in part or in whole. Also the said deputies shall have power to fine any that shall

be disorderly at their meetings, or for not coming in due time or place according to appointment; and they may return the said fines into the Court if it be refused to be paid, and the Treasurer to take notice of it, and to escheat or levy the same as he does other fines.

10. It is Ordered, sentenced, and decreed, that every General Court, except such as through neglect of the Governor and the greatest part of the Magistrates the Freemen themselves do call, shall consist of the Governor, or some one chosen to moderate the Court, and four other Magistrates at least, with the major part of the deputies of the several Towns legally chosen; and in case the Freemen, or major part of them, through neglect or refusal of the Governor and major part of the Magistrates, shall call a Court, it shall consist of the major part of Freemen that are present or their deputies, with a Moderator chosen by them: In which said General Courts shall consist the supreme power of the Commonwealth, and they only shall have power to make laws or repeal them, to grant levies, to admit of Freemen, dispose of lands undisposed of, to several Towns or persons, and also shall have power to call either Court or Magistrate or any other person whatsoever into question for any misdemeanor, and may for just causes displace or deal otherwise according to the nature of the offense; and also may deal in any other matter that concerns the good of this Commonwealth, except election of Magistrates, which shall be done by the whole body of Freemen.

In which Court the Governor or Moderator shall have power to order the Court, to give liberty of speech, and silence unseasonable and disorderly speakings, to put all things to vote, and in case the vote be equal to have the casting voice. But none of these Courts shall be adjourned or dissolved without the consent of the major part of the Court.

11. It is Ordered, sentenced, and decreed, that when any General Court upon the occasions of the Commonwealth have agreed upon any sum, or sums of money to be levied upon the several Towns within this Jurisdiction, that a committee be chosen to set out and appoint what shall be the proportion of every Town to pay of the said levy, provided the committee be made up of an equal number out of each Town.

14th January 1639 the 11 Orders above said are voted.

References

1   The January 14, 1638 date was in the old style Julian Calendar, before conversion to the modern new style Gregorian Calendar.

2   "Fundamental Orders." *The Columbia Encyclopedia, Sixth Edition*. Columbia University Press. 2005.

3   Lutz, Donald S.; Schechter, Stephen L.; Bernstein, Richard J. (1990). *Roots of the Republic: American founding documents interpreted*. Madison, Wis: Madison House. Pp. 24. ISBN 0-945612-19-2.

4   Secretary of the State of Connecticut (2007). "STATE OF CONNECTICUT Sites Seals Symbols." *The Connecticut State Register and Manual. State of Connecticut.*"

5   Horton, Wesley W. (1993-06-30). *The Connecticut State Constitution: A Reference Guide.* Reference guides to the state constitutions of the United States. No. 17. Westport, Connecticut: Greenwood Press. pp. 2.

6   Taylor, John M. *Roger Ludlow: The Colonial Lawmaker.* G.P. Putnam's Sons, New York, NY, 1990.

LESSON THREE

THE DECLARATION AND RESOLVES OF THE FIRST CONTINENTAL CONGRESS

Declaration and Resolves of the First Continental Congress

(October 14, 1774)

Continental Congress

▌The History[3*]

The first Continental Congress met in Carpenter's Hall in Philadelphia, from September 5, to October 26, 1774. Carpenter's Hall was also the seat of the Pennsylvania Congress. All of the colonies except Georgia sent delegates. These were elected by the people, by the colonial legislatures, or by the committees of correspondence of the respective colonies. The colonies presented there were united in a determination to show a combined authority to Great Britain, but their aims were not uniform at all. Pennsylvania and New York sent delegates with firm instructions to seek a resolution with England. The other colonies' voices were defensive of colonial rights, but pretty evenly divided between those who sought legislative parity, and the more radical members who were prepared for separation. Virginia's delegation was made up of a most even mix of these and, not coincidentally, presented the most eminent group of men in America: Colo. George Washington, Richard Henry Lee, Patrick Henry, Edmund Pendelton, Colo. Benjamin Harrison, Richard Bland, and at the head of them Peyton Randolph – who would immediately be elected president of the convention.

The objectives of the body were not entirely clear but, with such leadership as was found there, a core set of tasks was carried out. It was agreeable to all that the King and Parliament must be made to understand the grievances of the colonies and that the body must do everything possible to communicate the same to the population of America, and to the rest of the world.

The first few weeks were consumed in discussion and debate. The colonies had always, up to this time, acted as independent entities. There was much distrust to overcome. The first matter to be considered by all was A Plan of Union of Great Britain and the Colonies, offered by Joseph Galloway of Pennsylvania. The plan was considered very attractive to most of the members, as it proposed a popularly elected *Grand Council* which would represent the interests of the colonies as a whole, and would be a continental equivalent to the English Parliament. Poised against this would be a *President General*, appointed by the crown, to represent the authority of the king in America. Conflict in Boston overcame the effort at conciliation. The arrival of the Suffolk County (Boston) resolves just prior to the vote on the Plan of Union caused it to be discarded by a narrow margin.

On October 14, the Declaration and Resolves established the course of the congress, as a

---

[3] * Originally published as "First Continental Congress," *United States History*, Independence Hall Association, Carpenter's Hall, Philadelphia, Pennsylvania, 2008. For additional information see "The American Revolution, 1763–1783: The Colonies Move Toward Open Rebellion, 1773–1774," *American Memory Timeline*, Library of Congress, Washington, DC, 2003. This agency is listed in the *National Resource Directory* section of this volume.

statement of principles common to all of the colonies. Congress voted to meet again the following year if these grievances were not attended to by England.

▍The Document

Declaration and Resolves of the First Continental Congress

Whereas, since the close of the last war, the British parliament, claiming a power, of right, to bind the people of America by statutes in all cases whatsoever, hath, in some acts, expressly imposed taxes on them, and in others, under various presences, but in fact for the purpose of raising a revenue, hath imposed rates and duties payable in these colonies, established a board of commissioners, with unconstitutional powers, and extended the jurisdiction of courts of admiralty, not only for collecting the said duties, but for the trial of causes merely arising within the body of a county:

And whereas, in consequence of other statutes, judges, who before held only estates at will in their offices, have been made dependant on the crown alone for their salaries, and standing armies kept in times of peace: And whereas it has lately been resolved in parliament, that by force of a statute, made in the thirty-fifth year of the reign of King Henry the Eighth, colonists may be transported to England, and tried there upon accusations for treasons and misprisions, or concealments of treasons committed in the colonies, and by a late statute, such trials have been directed in cases therein mentioned:

And whereas, in the last session of parliament, three statutes were made; one entitled, "An act to discontinue, in such manner and for such time as are therein mentioned, the landing and discharging, lading, or shipping of goods, wares and merchandise, at the town, and within the harbour of Boston, in the province of Massachusetts-Bay in New England"; another entitled, "An act for the better regulating the government of the province of Massachusetts-Bay in New England;" and another entitled, "An act for the impartial administration of justice, in the cases of persons questioned for any act done by them in the execution of the law, or for the suppression of riots and tumults, in the province of the Massachusetts-Bay in New England;" and another statute was then made, "for making more effectual provision for the government of the province of Quebec, etc." All which statutes are impolitic, unjust, and cruel, as well as unconstitutional, and most dangerous and destructive of American rights:

And whereas, assemblies have been frequently dissolved, contrary to the rights of the people, when they attempted to deliberate on grievances; and their dutiful, humble, loyal, and reasonable petitions to the crown for redress, have been repeatedly treated with contempt, by his Majesty's ministers of state:

The good people of the several colonies of New-Hampshire, Massachusetts-Bay, Rhode Island and Providence Plantations, Connecticut, New-York, New-Jersey, Pennsylvania, Newcastle, Kent, and Sussex on Delaware, Maryland, Virginia, North-Carolina and South-Carolina, justly alarmed at these arbitrary proceedings of parliament and administration, have severally elected, constituted, and appointed deputies to meet, and sit in general Congress, in the city of Philadelphia, in order to obtain such establishment, as that their religion, laws, and liberties, may not be subverted: Whereupon the deputies so appointed being now assembled, in a full and free representation of these colonies, taking into their most serious consideration, the best means of attaining the ends aforesaid, do, in the first place, as Englishmen, their ancestors in like cases have usually done, for asserting and vindicating their rights and liberties, DECLARE,

That the inhabitants of the English colonies in North-America, by the immutable laws of nature, the principles of the English constitution, and the several charters or compacts, have the following RIGHTS:

Resolved, N.C.D. 1. That they are entitled to life, liberty and property: and they have never ceded to any foreign power whatever, a right to dispose of either without their consent.

Resolved, N.C.D. 2. That our ancestors, who first settled these colonies, were at the time of their emigration from the mother country, entitled to all the rights, liberties, and immunities of free and natural-born subjects, within the realm of England.

Resolved, N.C.D. 3. That by such emigration they by no means forfeited, surrendered, or lost any of those rights, but that they were, and their descendants now are, entitled to the exercise and enjoyment of all such of them, as their local and other circumstances enable them to exercise and enjoy.

Resolved, 4. That the foundation of English liberty, and of all free government, is a right in the people to participate in their legislative council: and as the English colonists are not represented, and from their local and other circumstances, cannot properly be represented in the British parliament, they are entitled to a free and exclusive power of legislation in their several provincial legislatures, where their right of representation can alone be preserved, in all cases of taxation and internal polity, subject only to the negative of their sovereign, in such manner as has been heretofore used and accustomed: But, from the necessity of the case, and a regard to the mutual interest of both countries, we cheerfully consent to the operation of such acts of the British parliament, as are bonfide, restrained to the regulation of our external commerce, for the purpose of securing the commercial advantages of the whole empire to the mother country, and the commercial benefits of its respective members; excluding every idea of taxation internal or external, for raising a revenue on the subjects, in America, without their consent.

Resolved, N.C.D. 5. That the respective colonies are entitled to the common law of England, and more especially to the great and inestimable privilege of being tried by their peers of the vicinage, according to the course of that law.

Resolved, N.C.D. 6. That they are entitled to the benefit of such of the English statutes, as existed at the time of their colonization; and which they have, by experience, respectively found to be applicable to their several local and other circumstances.

Resolved, N.C.D. 7. That these, his Majesty's colonies, are likewise entitled to all the immunities and privileges granted and confirmed to them by royal charters, or secured by their several codes of provincial laws.

Resolved, N.C.D. 8. That they have a right peaceably to assemble, consider of their grievances, and petition the king; and that all prosecutions, prohibitory proclamations, and commitments for the same, are illegal.

Resolved, N.C.D. 9. That the keeping a standing army in these colonies, in times of peace, without the consent of the legislature of that colony, in which such army is kept, is against law.

Resolved, N.C.D. 10. It is indispensably necessary to good government, and rendered essential by the English constitution, that the constituent branches of the legislature be independent of each other; that, therefore, the exercise of legislative power in several colonies, by a council appointed, during pleasure, by the crown, is unconstitutional, dangerous and destructive to the freedom of American legislation.

All and each of which the aforesaid deputies, in behalf of themselves, and their constituents, do claim, demand, and insist on, as their indubitable rights and liberties, which cannot be legally taken from them, altered or abridged by any power whatever, without their own consent, by their representatives in their several provincial legislatures.

In the course of our inquiry, we find many infringements and violations of the foregoing rights, which, from an ardent desire, that harmony and mutual intercourse of affection and interest may be restored, we pass over for the present, and proceed to state such acts and measures as have been adopted since the last war, which demonstrate a system formed to enslave America.

Resolved, N.C.D. That the following acts of parliament are infringements and violations of the rights of the colonists; and that the repeal of them is essentially necessary, in order to restore harmony between Great Britain and the American colonies, viz.

The several acts of Geo. III. ch. 15, and ch. 34.-5 Geo. III. ch. 25.-6 Geo. ch. 52.-7 Geo. III. ch. 41 and ch. 46.-8 Geo. III. ch. 22. which impose duties for the purpose of raising a revenue in America, extend the power of the admiralty courts beyond their ancient limits, deprive the American subject of trial by jury, authorize the judges certificate to indemnify the prosecutor from damages, that he might otherwise be liable to, requiring oppressive security from a claimant of ships and goods seized, before he shall be allowed to defend his property, and are subversive of American rights.

Also 12 Geo. III. ch. 24, intituled, "An act for the better securing his majesty's dockyards, magazines, ships, ammunition, and stores," which declares a new offence in America, and deprives the American subject of a constitutional trial by jury of the vicinage, by authorizing the trial of any person, charged with the committing any offence described in the said act, out of the realm, to be indicted and tried for the same in any shire or county within the realm.

Also the three acts passed in the last session of parliament, for stopping the port and blocking up the harbour of Boston, for altering the charter and government of Massachusetts-Bay, and that which is entitled, "An act for the better administration of justice, etc."

Also the act passed in the same session for establishing the Roman Catholic religion, in the province of Quebec, abolishing the equitable system of English laws, and erecting a tyranny there, to the great danger (from so total a dissimilarity of religion, law and government) of the neighboring British colonies, by the assistance of whose blood and treasure the said country was conquered from France.

Also the act passed in the same session, for the better providing suitable quarters for officers and soldiers in his majesty's service, in North-America.

Also, that the keeping a standing army in several of these colonies, in time of peace, without the consent of the legislature of that colony, in which such army is kept, is against law.

To these grievous acts and measures, Americans cannot submit, but in hopes their fellow subjects in Great Britain will, on a revision of them, restore us to that state, in which both countries found happiness and prosperity, we have for the present, only resolved to pursue the following peaceable measures: 1. To enter into a non-importation, non-consumption, and non-exportation agreement or association. 2. To prepare an address to the people of Great-Britain, and a memorial to the inhabitants of British America: and 3. To prepare a loyal address to his majesty, agreeable to resolutions already entered into.

LESSON FOUR

THE DECLARATION OF THE CAUSES AND NECESSITY OF TAKING UP ARMS

Declaration of the Causes and Necessity of Taking Up Arms

(July 6, 1775)

Continental Congress

The History[4*]

The Declaration of the Causes and Necessity of Taking Up Arms was a document issued by the Second Continental Congress on July 6, 1775, to explain why the Thirteen Colonies had taken up arms in what had become the American Revolutionary War, and represents an important development in the political thought that went into the American Revolution. The final draft of the Declaration was written by John Dickinson, who incorporated language from an earlier draft by Thomas Jefferson.

The Declaration describes what colonists viewed as the unconstitutional effort by the British Parliament to extend its jurisdiction into the colonies following the Seven Years' War. Objectionable policies listed in the Declaration include taxation without representation, extended use of vice admiralty courts, the several Coercive Acts, and the Declaratory Act. The Declaration describes how the colonists had, for ten years, repeatedly petitioned for the redress of their grievances, only to have their pleas ignored or rejected by the British monarchy and government. Even though British troops have been sent to enforce these unconstitutional acts, the Declaration insists that the colonists do not yet seek independence from the British Empire, only a self-governing place within it. They have taken up arms "in defence of the Freedom that is our Birthright and which we ever enjoyed until the late Violation of it," and will "lay them down when Hostilities shall cease on the part of the Aggressors."

In the 19th century, the authorship of the Declaration was disputed. In a collection of his works first published in 1801, John Dickinson took credit for writing the Declaration. This claim went unchallenged by Thomas Jefferson until many years later, when Jefferson was nearly 80 years old. In his autobiography, Jefferson claimed that he wrote the first draft, but Dickinson objected that it was too radical, and so Congress allowed Dickinson to write a more moderate version, keeping only the last four-and-a-half paragraphs of Jefferson's draft. Jefferson's version of events was accepted by historians for many years. In 1950, Julian P. Boyd, the editor of Jefferson's papers, examined the extant drafts and determined that Jefferson's memory was faulty and that Dickinson claimed too much credit for the final text.

According to Boyd, an initial draft was reportedly written by John Rutledge, a member of a committee of five appointed to create the Declaration. Rutledge's draft was not accepted and does

---

[4] * Originally published as "Declaration of the Causes and Necessity of Taking Up Arms," *Wikipedia*, Wikimedia Foundation, Inc., San Francisco, California, October 2009. For additional information see "The American Revolution, 1763–1783: First Shots of War, 1775," *American Memory Timeline*, Library of Congress, Washington, DC, 2003. This agency is listed in the *National Resource Directory* section of this volume.

not survive, Jefferson and Dickinson were then added to the committee. Jefferson was appointed to write a draft; how much he drew upon the lost Rutledge draft, if at all, is unknown. Jefferson then apparently submitted his draft to Dickinson, who suggested some changes, which Jefferson, for the most part, decided not to use. The result was that Dickinson rewrote the Declaration, keeping some passages written by Jefferson. Contrary to Jefferson's recollection in his old age, Dickinson's version was not less radical; according to Boyd, in some respects Dickinson's draft was more blunt. The bold statement near the end was written by Dickinson: "Our cause is just. Our union is perfect. Our internal resources are great, and, if necessary, foreign assistance is undoubtedly attainable." The disagreement in 1775 between Dickinson and Jefferson appears to have been primarily a matter of style, not content.

The Document

Declaration of the Causes and Necessity of Taking Up Arms[1]

If it was possible for men, who exercise their reason to believe, that the divine Author of our existence intended a part of the human race to hold an absolute property in, and an unbounded power over others, marked out by his infinite goodness and wisdom, as the objects of a legal domination never rightfully resistible, however severe and oppressive, the inhabitants of these colonies might at least require from the parliament of Great-Britain some evidence, that this dreadful authority over them, has been granted to that body. But a reverance for our Creator, principles of humanity, and the dictates of common sense, must convince all those who reflect upon the subject, that government was instituted to promote the welfare of mankind, and ought to be administered for the attainment of that end. The legislature of Great-Britain, however, stimulated by an inordinate passion for a power not only unjustifiable, but which they know to be peculiarly reprobated by the very constitution of that kingdom, and desparate of success in any mode of contest, where regard should be had to truth, law, or right, have at length, deserting those, attempted to effect their cruel and impolitic purpose of enslaving these colonies by violence, and have thereby rendered it necessary for us to close with their last appeal from reason to arms.– Yet, however blinded that assembly may be, by their intemperate rage for unlimited domination, so to sight justice and the opinion of mankind, we esteem ourselves bound by obligations of respect to the rest of the world, to make known the justice of our cause.

Our forefathers, inhabitants of the island of Great-Britain, left their native land, to seek on these shores a residence for civil and religious freedom. At the expense of their blood, at the hazard of their fortunes, without the least charge to the country from which they removed, by unceasing labour, and an unconquerable spirit, they effected settlements in the distant and unhospitable wilds of America, then filled with numerous and warlike barbarians. – Societies or governments, vested with perfect legislatures, were formed under charters from the crown, and an harmonious intercourse was established between the colonies and the kingdom from which they derived their origin. The mutual benefits of this union became in a short time so extraordinary, as to excite astonishment. It is universally confessed, that the amazing increase of the wealth, strength, and navigation of the realm, arose from this source; and the minister, who so wisely and successfully directed the measures of Great-Britain in the late war, publicly declared, that these colonies enabled her to triumph over her enemies. – Towards the conclusion of that war, it pleased our sovereign to make a change in his counsels. – From that fatal movement, the affairs of the British empire began to fall into confusion, and gradually sliding from the summit of glorious prosperity, to which they had been advanced by the virtues and abilities of one man, are at length distracted by the convulsions, that now shake it to its deepest foundations. – The new ministry finding the brave foes of Britain, though frequently defeated, yet still contending, took up the unfortunate idea of granting them a hasty peace, and then subduing her faithful friends.

These devoted colonies were judged to be in such a state, as to present victories without bloodshed, and all the easy emoluments of statuteable plunder. – The uninterrupted tenor of their peaceable and respectful behaviour from the beginning of colonization, their dutiful, zealous, and useful services during the war, though so recently and amply acknowledged in the most honourable manner by his majesty, by the late king, and by parliament, could not save them from the meditated innovations. – Parliament was influenced to adopt the pernicious project, and assuming a new power over them, have in the course of eleven years, given such decisive specimens of the spirit and consequences attending this power, as to leave no doubt concerning the effects of acquiescence under it. They have undertaken to give and grant our money without our consent, though we have ever exercised an exclusive right to dispose of our own property; statutes have been passed for extending the jurisdiction of courts of admiralty and vice-admiralty beyond their ancient limits; for depriving us of the accustomed and inestimable privilege of trial by jury, in cases affecting both life and property; for suspending the legislature of one of the colonies; for interdicting all commerce to the capital of another; and for altering fundamentally the form of government established by charter, and secured by acts of its own legislature solemnly confirmed by the crown; for exempting the "*murderers*" of colonists from legal trial, and in effect, from punishment; for erecting in a neighbouring province, acquired by the joint arms of Great-Britain and America, a despotism dangerous to our very existence; and for quartering soldiers upon the colonists in time of profound peace. It has also been resolved in parliament, that colonists charged with committing certain offences, shall be transported to England to be tried.

But why should we enumerate our injuries in detail? By one statute it is declared, that parliament can "*of right make laws to bind us in all cases whatsoever.*" What is to defend us against so enormous, so unlimited a power? Not a single man of those who assume it, is chosen by us; or is subject to our control or influence; but, on the contrary, they are all of them exempt from the operation of such laws, and an American revenue, if not diverted from the ostensible purposes for which it is raised, would actually lighten their own burdens in proportion, as they increase ours. We saw the misery to which such despotism would reduce us. We for ten years incessantly and ineffectually besieged the throne as supplicants; we reasoned, we remonstrated with parliament, in the most mild and decent language.

Administration sensible that we should regard these oppressive measures as freemen ought to do, sent over fleets and armies to enforce them. The indignation of the Americans was roused, it is true; but it was the indignation of a virtuous, loyal, and affectionate people. A Congress of delegates from the United Colonies was assembled at Philadelphia, on the fifth day of last September. We resolved again to offer an humble and dutiful petition to the King, and also addressed our fellow-subjects of Great-Britain. We have pursued every temperate, every respectful measure; we have even proceeded to break off our commercial intercourse with our fellow-subjects, as the last peaceable admonition, that our attachment to no nation upon earth should supplant our attachment to liberty.– This, we flattered ourselves, was the ultimate step of the controversy: but subsequent events have shewn, how vain was this hope of finding moderation in our enemies.

Several threatening expressions against the colonies were inserted in his majesty's speech; our petition, tho' we were told it was a decent one, and that his majesty had been pleased to receive it graciously, and to promise laying it before his parliament, was huddled into both houses among a bundle of American papers, and there neglected. The lords and commons in their address, in the month of February, said, that *"a rebellion at that time actually existed within the province of Massachusetts-Bay; and that those concerned with it, had been countenanced and encouraged by unlawful combinations and engagements, entered into by his majesty's subjects in several of the other colonies; and therefore they besought his majesty, that he would take the most effectual measures to inforce due obediance to the laws and authority of the supreme legislature."*– Soon after, the commercial intercourse of whole colonies, with foreign countries, and with each other, was cut off by an act of parliament; by another several of them were intirely prohibited from the fisheries in the seas near their coasts, on which they always depended for their sustenance; and large reinforcements of ships and troops were immediately sent over to general Gage.

Fruitless were all the entreaties, arguments, and eloquence of an illustrious band of the most distinguished peers, and commoners, who nobly and strenuously asserted the justice of our cause, to stay, or even to mitigate the heedless fury with which these accumulated and unexampled outrages were hurried on.– Equally fruitless was the interference of the city of London, of Bristol, and many other respectable towns in our favor. Parliament adopted an insidious manoeuvre calculated to divide us, to establish a perpetual auction of taxations where colony should bid against colony, all of them uninformed what ransom would redeem their lives; and thus to extort from us, at the point of the bayonet, the unknown sums that should be sufficient to gratify, if possible to gratify, ministerial rapacity, with the miserable indulgence left to us of raising, in our own mode, the prescribed tribute. What terms more rigid and humiliating could have been dictated by remorseless victors to conquered enemies? In our circumstances to accept them, would be to deserve them.

Soon after the intelligence of these proceedings arrived on this continent, general Gage, who in the course of the last year had taken possession of the town of Boston, in the province of Massachusetts-Bay, and still occupied it a garrison, on the 19th day of April, sent out from that place a large detachment of his army, who made an unprovoked assault on the inhabitants of the said province, at the town of Lexington, as appears by the affidavits of a great number of persons, some of whom were officers and soldiers of that detachment, murdered eight of the inhabitants, and wounded many others. From thence the troops proceeded in warlike array to the town of Concord, where they set upon another party of the inhabitants of the same province, killing several and wounding more, until compelled to retreat by the country people suddenly assembled to repel this cruel aggression. Hostilities, thus commenced by the British troops, have been since prosecuted by them without regard to faith or reputation.– The inhabitants of Boston being confined within that town by the general their governor, and having, in order to procure their dismission, entered into a treaty with him, it was stipulated that the said inhabitants having deposited their arms with their own magistrate, should have liberty to depart, taking with them their other effects. They accordingly delivered up their arms, but in open violation of honour, in defiance of the obligation of treaties, which even savage nations esteemed sacred, the governor ordered the arms deposited as aforesaid, that they might be preserved for their owners, to be seized by a body of soldiers; detained the greatest part of the inhabitants in the town, and compelled the few who were permitted to retire, to leave their most valuable effects behind.

By this perfidy wives are separated from their husbands, children from their parents, the aged and the sick from their relations and friends, who wish to attend and comfort them; and those who have been used to live in plenty and even elegance, are reduced to deplorable distress.

The general, further emulating his ministerial masters, by a proclamation bearing date on the 12th day of June, after venting the grossest falsehoods and calumnies against the good people of these colonies, proceeds to *"declare them all, either by name or description, to be rebels and traitors, to supersede the course of the common law, and instead thereof to publish and order the use and exercise of the law martial."*– His troops have butchered our countrymen, have wantonly burnt Charlestown, besides a considerable number of houses in other places; our ships and vessels are seized; the necessary supplies of provisions are intercepted, and he is exerting his utmost power to spread destruction and devastation around him.

We have received certain intelligence, that general Carelton *[Carleton]*, the governor of Canada, is instigating the people of that province and the Indians to fall upon us; and we have but too much reason to apprehend, that schemes have been formed to excite domestic enemies against us. In brief, a part of these colonies now feel, and all of them are sure of feeling, as far as the vengeance of administration can inflict them, the complicated calamities of fire, sword and famine. We[2] are reduced to the alternative of chusing an unconditional submission to the tyranny of irritated ministers, or resistance by force .– The latter is our choice.– We have counted the cost of this contest, and find nothing so dreadful as voluntary slavery.– Honour, justice, and humanity, forbid us tamely to surrender that freedom which we received from our gallant ancestors, and which our innocent posterity have a right to receive from us. We cannot endure the infamy and guilt of resigning succeeding generations to that wretchedness which inevitably awaits them, if we basely entail hereditary bondage upon them.

Our cause is just. Our union is perfect. Our internal resources are great, and, if necessary, foreign assistance is undoubtedly attainable .– We gratefully acknowledge, as signal instances of the Divine favour towards us, that his Providence would not permit us to be called into this severe controversy, until we were grown up to our present strength, had been previously exercised in warlike operation, and possessed of the means of defending ourselves. With hearts fortified with these animating reflections, we most solemnly, before God and the world, declare, that, exerting the utmost energy of those powers, which our beneficent Creator hath graciously bestowed upon us, the arms we have been compelled by our enemies to assume, we will, in defiance of every hazard, with unabating firmness and perseverence, employ for the preservation of our liberties; being with one mind resolved to die freemen rather than to live slaves.

Lest this declaration should disquiet the minds of our friends and fellow-subjects in any part of the empire, we assure them that we mean not to dissolve that union which has so long and so happily subsisted between us, and which we sincerely wish to see restored.– Necessity has not yet driven us into that desperate measure, or induced us to excite any other nation to war against them.– We have not raised armies with ambitious designs of separating from Great-Britain, and establishing independent states. We fight not for glory or for conquest. We exhibit to mankind the remarkable spectacle of a people attacked by unprovoked enemies, without any imputation or even suspicion of offence. They boast of their privileges and civilization, and yet proffer no milder conditions than servitude or death.

In our own native land, in defense of the freedom that is our birthright, and which we ever enjoyed till the late violation of it – for the protection of our property, acquired solely by the honest industry of our fore-fathers and ourselves, against violence actually offered, we have taken up arms. We shall lay them down when hostilities shall cease on the part of the aggressors, and all danger of their being renewed shall be removed, and not before.

With a humble confidence in the mercies of the supreme and impartial Judge and Ruler of the Universe, we most devoutly implore his divine goodness to protect us happily through this great conflict, to dispose our adversaries to reconciliation on reasonable terms, and thereby to relieve the empire from the calamities of civil war.

REFERENCES

1   Primarily the work of Thomas Jefferson and John Dickinson. p. 168 Morison, Samuel Eliot, Henry Steele Commager, and William E. Leuchtenburg. *The Growth of the American Republic: Volume 1.* Seventh Edition. New York: Oxford University Press; 1980. (Note added by the Avalon Project.)

2   From this point the declaration follows Jefferson's draft.

LESSON FIVE

THE VIRGINIA DECLARATION OF RIGHTS

Virginia Declaration of Rights

(June 12, 1776)

House of Burgesses

The History[5][*]

The Virginia Declaration of Rights is a document drafted in 1776 to proclaim the inherent natural rights of men, including the right to rebel against "inadequate" government. It influenced a number of later documents, including the United States Declaration of Independence (1776), the United States Bill of Rights (1789), and the French Revolution's Declaration of the Rights of Man and of the Citizen (1789). The Declaration was adopted unanimously by the Virginia Convention of Delegates on June 12, 1776 as a separate document from the Constitution of Virginia adopted on June 29, 1776.[1] It was later incorporated within the Virginia State Constitution as Article I, and a slightly updated version may still be seen in Virginia's Constitution, making it legally in effect to this day.

It was initially drafted by George Mason *ca.* May 20-26, 1776, and later amended by Thomas Ludwell Lee and the Convention to add Section 14 on the right to uniform government. Mason based his document on the rights of citizens described in earlier works such as the English Bill of Rights (1689), and the Declaration can be considered the first modern Constitutional protection of individual rights for citizens of North America. It rejected the notion of privileged political classes or hereditary offices such as the members of Parliament and House of Lords described in the English Bill of Rights.

The Declaration consists of sixteen articles on the subject of which rights "pertain to [the people of Virginia] … as the basis and foundation of Government."[1] In addition to affirming the inherent nature of natural rights to life, liberty, and property, the Declaration both describes a view of Government as the servant of the people, and enumerates various restrictions on governmental power. Thus, the document is unusual in that it not only prescribes legal rights, but it also describes moral principles upon which a government should be run.[2]

The Virginia Declaration of Rights heavily influenced later documents. Thomas Jefferson is thought to have drawn on it when he drafted the United States Declaration of Independence one month later (July 1776). James Madison was also influenced by the Declaration while drafting the Bill of Rights (completed September 1787, approved 1789), as was the Marquis de Lafayette in voting the French Revolution's Declaration of the Rights of Man and of the Citizen (1789).

The importance of the Virginia Declaration of Rights is that it was the first constitutional

---

[5] [*] Originally published as "Virginia Declaration of Rights," *Wikipedia*, Wikimedia Foundation, Inc., San Francisco, California, November 2009. For additional information see "The Virginia Declaration of Rights," *American Treasurers of the Library of Congress*, Library of Congress, Washington, DC, 2002. This agency is listed in the *National Resource Directory* section of this volume.

protection of individual rights, rather than protecting just members of Parliament or consisting of simple laws that can be changed as easily as passed.

The Document

Virginia Declaration of Rights

I. That all men are by nature equally free and independent, and have certain inherent rights, of which, when they enter into a state of society, they cannot, by any compact, deprive or divest their posterity; namely, the enjoyment of life and liberty, with the means of acquiring and possessing property, and pursuing and obtaining happiness and safety.

II. That all power is vested in, and consequently derived from, the people; that magistrates are their trustees and servants, and at all times amenable to them.

III. That government is, or ought to be, instituted for the common benefit, protection, and security of the people, nation or community; of all the various modes and forms of government that is best, which is capable of producing the greatest degree of happiness and safety and is most effectually secured against the danger of maladministration; and that, whenever any government shall be found inadequate or contrary to these purposes, a majority of the community hath an indubitable, unalienable, and indefeasible right to reform, alter or abolish it, in such manner as shall be judged most conducive to the public weal.

IV. That no man, or set of men, are entitled to exclusive or separate emoluments or privileges from the community, but in consideration of public services; which, not being descendible, neither ought the offices of magistrate, legislator, or judge be hereditary.

V. That the legislative and executive powers of the state should be separate and distinct from the judicative; and, that the members of the two first may be restrained from oppression by feeling and participating the burthens of the people, they should, at fixed periods, be reduced to a private station, return into that body from which they were originally taken, and the vacancies be supplied by frequent, certain, and regular elections in which all, or any part of the former members, to be again eligible, or ineligible, as the laws shall direct.

VI. That elections of members to serve as representatives of the people in assembly ought to be free; and that all men, having sufficient evidence of permanent common interest with, and attachment to, the community have the right of suffrage and cannot be taxed or deprived of their property for public uses without their own consent or that of their representatives so elected, nor bound by any law to which they have not, in like manner, assented, for the public good.

VII. That all power of suspending laws, or the execution of laws, by any authority without consent of the representatives of the people is injurious to their rights and ought not to be exercised.

VIII. That in all capital or criminal prosecutions a man hath a right to demand the cause and nature of his accusation to be confronted with the accusers and witnesses, to call for evidence in his favor, and to a speedy trial by an impartial jury of his vicinage, without whose unanimous consent he cannot be found guilty, nor can he be compelled to give evidence against himself; that no man be deprived of his liberty except by the law of the land or the judgement of his peers.

IX. That excessive bail ought not to be required, nor excessive fines imposed; nor cruel and unusual punishments inflicted.

X. That general warrants, whereby any officer or messenger may be commanded to search suspected places without evidence of a fact committed, or to seize any person or persons not named, or whose offense is not particularly described and supported by evidence, are grievous and oppressive and ought not to be granted.

XI. That in controversies respecting property and in suits between man and man, the ancient trial by jury is preferable to any other and ought to be held sacred.

XII. That the freedom of the press is one of the greatest bulwarks of liberty and can never be restrained but by despotic governments.

XIII. That a well regulated militia, composed of the body of the people, trained to arms, is the proper, natural, and safe defense of a free state; that standing armies, in time of peace, should be avoided as dangerous to liberty; and that, in all cases, the military should be under strict subordination to, and be governed by, the civil power.

XIV. That the people have a right to uniform government; and therefore, that no government separate from, or independent of, the government of Virginia, ought to be erected or established within the limits thereof.

XV. That no free government, or the blessings of liberty, can be preserved to any people but by a firm adherence to justice, moderation, temperance, frugality, and virtue and by frequent recurrence to fundamental principles.

XVI. That religion, or the duty which we owe to our Creator and the manner of discharging it, can be directed by reason and conviction, not by force or violence; and therefore, all men are equally entitled to the free exercise of religion, according to the dictates of conscience; and that it is the mutual duty of all to practice Christian forbearance, love, and charity towards each other.

Adopted unanimously June 12, 1776 Virginia Convention of Delegates drafted by Mr. George Mason.

References

1   Primarily the work of Thomas Jefferson and John Dickinson. p. 168 Morison, Samuel Eliot, Henry Steele Commager, and William E. Leuchtenburg. *The Growth of the American Republic:* Volume 1. Seventh Edition. New York: Oxford University Press; 1980. (Note added by the Avalon Project.)

2   From this point the declaration follows Jefferson's draft.

LESSON SIX

THE DECLARATION OF INDEPENDENCE

Declaration of Independence

(July 4, 1776)

Continental Congress

▌The History[6*]

Since its creation in 1776, the Declaration of Independence has been considered the single most important expression of the ideals of U.S. democracy. As a statement of the fundamental principles of the United States, the Declaration is an enduring reminder of the country's commitment to popular government and equal rights for all.

The Declaration of Independence is a product of the early days of the Revolutionary War. On July 2, 1776, the Second Continental Congress – the legislature of the American colonies – voted for independence from Great Britain. It then appointed a committee of five – John Adams, Benjamin Franklin, Thomas Jefferson, Roger Sherman, and Robert R. Livingston – to draft a formal statement of independence designed to influence public opinion at home and abroad. Because of his reputation as an eloquent and forceful writer, Jefferson was assigned the task of creating the document, and the final product is almost entirely his own work. The Congress did not approve all of Jefferson's original draft, however, rejecting most notably his denunciation of the slave trade. Delegates from South Carolina and Georgia were not yet ready to extend the notion of inalienable rights to African Americans.

On July 4, 1776, the day of birth for the new country, the Continental Congress approved the Declaration of Independence on behalf of the people living in the American colonies. The Declaration served a number of purposes for the newly formed United States. With regard to the power politics of the day, it functioned as a propaganda statement intended to build support for American independence abroad, particularly in France, from which the Americans hoped to have support in their struggle for independence. Similarly, it served as a clear message of intention to the British. Even more important for the later Republic of the United States, it functioned as a statement of governmental ideals.

In keeping with its immediate diplomatic purposes, most of the Declaration consists of a list of 30 grievances against acts of the British monarch George III. Many of these were traditional and legitimate grievances under British Constitutional Law. The Declaration firmly announces that British actions had established "an absolute Tyranny over these States." Britain's acts of despotism, according to the Declaration's list, included taxation of Americans without representation in Parliament; imposition of standing armies on American communities; establishment of the military

---

6 * Originally published as "Declaration of Independence – Further Readings," *American Law and Legal Encyclopedia*, Net Industries, LLC, Savoy, Illinois, 2009. For additional information see "The History of the Declaration of Independence," *The Charters of Freedom*, U.S. National Archives and Records Administration, College Park, Maryland, 2004. This agency is listed in the *National Resource Directory* section of this volume.

above the civil power; obstruction of the right to trial by jury; interference with the operation of colonial legislatures; and cutting off of trade with the rest of the world. The Declaration ends with the decisive resolution that "these United Colonies are, and of Right ought to be Free and Independent States; that they are Absolved from all Allegiance to the British Crown, and that all political connection between them and the State of Great Britain, is and ought to be totally dissolved."

The first sentences of the document and their statement of political ideals have remained the Declaration's most memorable and influential section.

Ever since their creation, these ideas have guided the development of U.S. government, including the creation of the U.S. Constitution in 1787. The concepts of equal and inalienable rights for all, limited government, popular consent, and freedom to rebel have had a lasting effect on U.S. law and politics.

The Document

Declaration of Independence[1] [2]

When in the course of human events, it becomes necessary for one people to dissolve the political bands which have connected them with another, and to assume among the powers of the earth, the separate and equal station to which the laws of nature and of nature's God entitle them, a decent respect to the opinions of mankind requires that they should declare the causes which impel them to the separation. We hold these truths to be self-evident:

That all men are created equal; that they are endowed by their Creator with certain unalienable rights; that among these are life, liberty, and the pursuit of happiness; that, to secure these rights, governments are instituted among men, deriving their just powers from the consent of the governed; that whenever any form of government becomes destructive of these ends, it is the right of the people to alter or to abolish it, and to institute new government, laying its foundation on such principles, and organizing its powers in such form, as to them shall seem most likely to effect their safety and happiness. Prudence, indeed, will dictate that governments long established should not be changed for light and transient causes; and accordingly all experience hath shown that mankind are more disposed to suffer, while evils are sufferable than to right themselves by abolishing the forms to which they are accustomed. But when a long train of abuses and usurpations, pursuing invariably the same object, evinces a design to reduce them under absolute despotism, it is their right, it is their duty, to throw off such government, and to provide new guards for their future security. Such has been the patient sufferance of these colonies; and such is now the necessity which constrains them to alter their former systems of government. The history of the present King of Great Britain is a history of repeated injuries and usurpations, all having in direct object the establishment of an absolute tyranny over these states. To prove this, let facts be submitted to a candid world.

He has refused his assent to laws, the most wholesome and necessary for the public good.

He has forbidden his governors to pass laws of immediate and pressing importance, unless suspended in their operation till his assent should be obtained; and, when so suspended, he has utterly neglected to attend to them.

He has refused to pass other laws for the accommodation of large districts of people, unless those people would relinquish the right of representation in the legislature, a right inestimable to them, and formidable to tyrants only.

He has called together legislative bodies at places unusual uncomfortable, and distant from the depository of their public records, for the sole purpose of fatiguing them into compliance with his measures.

He has dissolved representative houses repeatedly, for opposing, with manly firmness, his invasions on the rights of the people.

He has refused for a long time, after such dissolutions, to cause others to be elected; whereby the legislative powers, incapable of annihilation, have returned to the people at large for their exercise; the state remaining, in the mean time, exposed to all the dangers of invasions from without and convulsions within.

He has endeavored to prevent the population of these states; for that purpose obstructing the laws for naturalization of foreigners; refusing to pass others to encourage their migration hither, and raising the conditions of new appropriations of lands.

He has obstructed the administration of justice, by refusing his assent to laws for establishing judiciary powers.

He has made judges dependent on his will alone, for the tenure of their offices, and the amount and payment of their salaries.

He has erected a multitude of new offices, and sent hither swarms of officers to harass our people and eat out their substance.

He has kept among us, in times of peace, standing armies, without the consent of our legislatures.

He has affected to render the military independent of, and superior to, the civil power.

He has combined with others to subject us to a jurisdiction foreign to our Constitution and unacknowledged by our laws, giving his assent to their acts of pretended legislation:

For quartering large bodies of armed troops among us;

For protecting them, by a mock trial, from punishment for any murders which they should commit on the inhabitants of these states;

For cutting off our trade with all parts of the world;

For imposing taxes on us without our consent;

For depriving us, in many cases, of the benefits of trial by jury;

For transporting us beyond seas, to be tried for pretended offenses;

For abolishing the free system of English laws in a neighboring province, establishing therein an arbitrary government, and enlarging its boundaries, so as to render it at once an example and fit instrument for introducing the same absolute rule into these colonies;

For taking away our charters, abolishing our most valuable laws, and altering fundamentally the forms of our governments;

For suspending our own legislatures, and declaring themselves invested with power to legislate for us in all cases whatsoever.

He has abdicated government here, by declaring us out of his protection and waging war against us.

He has plundered our seas, ravaged our coasts, burned our towns, and destroyed the lives of our people.

He is at this time transporting large armies of foreign mercenaries to complete the works of death, desolation, and tyranny already begun with circumstances of cruelty and perfidy scarcely paralleled in the most barbarous ages, and totally unworthy the head of a civilized nation.

He has constrained our fellow-citizens, taken captive on the high seas, to bear arms against their country, to become the executioners of their friends and brethren, or to fall themselves by their hands.

He has excited domestic insurrection among us, and has endeavored to bring on the inhabitants of our frontiers the merciless Indian savages, whose known rule of warfare is an undistinguished destruction of all ages, sexes, and conditions.

In every stage of these oppressions we have petitioned for redress in the most humble terms; our repeated petitions have been answered only by repeated injury. A prince, whose character is thus marked by every act which may define a tyrant, is unfit to be the ruler of a free people.

Nor have we been wanting in our attentions to our British brethren. We have warned them, from time to time, of attempts by their legislature to extend an unwarrantable jurisdiction over us. We have reminded them of the circumstances of our emigration and settlement here. We have appealed to their native justice and magnanimity; and we have conjured them, by the ties of our common kindred, to disavow these usurpations which would inevitably interrupt our connections and correspondence. They too, have been deaf to the voice of justice and of consanguinity. We must, therefore, acquiesce in the necessity which denounces our separation, and hold them as we hold the rest of mankind, enemies in war, in peace friends.

We, therefore, the representatives of the United States of America, in General Congress assembled, appealing to the Supreme Judge of the world for the rectitude of our intentions, do, in the name and by the authority of the good people of these colonies solemnly publish and declare, That these United Colonies are, and of right ought to be, FREE AND INDEPENDENT STATES; that they are absolved from all allegiance to the British crown and that all political connection between them and the state of Great Britain is, and ought to be, totally dissolved; and that, as free and independent states, they have full power to levy war, conclude peace, contract alliances, establish commerce, and do all other acts and things which independent states may of right do. And for the support of this declaration, with a firm reliance on the protection of Divine Providence, we mutually pledge to each other our lives, our fortunes, and our sacred honor.

– [Signed by] JOHN HANCOCK
[President]

REFERENCES

1   Mr. Ferdinand Jefferson, Keeper of the Rolls in the Department of State, at Washington, says: "The names of the signers are spelt above as in the facsimile of the original, but the punctuation of them is not always the same; neither do the names of the Sates appear in the facsimile of the original. The names of the signers of each State are grouped together in the facsimile of the original, except the name of Matthew Thornton, which follows that of Oliver Wolcott." — Revised Statutes of the United States, 2d edition, 1878, p. 6.

2   The first local government in the American colonies to declare its independence from Great Britain was Mecklenburg County, North Carolina, on May 20, 1775. The county declared its independence from Great Britain immediately after the Battle of Lexington, in what is now called the Commonwealth of Massachusetts. Additional information concerning the "Mecklenburg Declaration of Independence" can be found on the Library of Congress website, which is listed in the *National Resource Directory* section of this volume. Because of its significance, this document is shown in its entirety in the Appendix of this volume under the heading "Local Government Historical Document."

LESSON SEVEN

THE CONSTITUTION OF MASSACHUSETTS

Constitution of Massachusetts

(June 15, 1780)

State Constitutional Convention Representatives

The History[7][*]

The Constitution of the Commonwealth of Massachusetts is the fundamental governing document of the Commonwealth of Massachusetts, one of the 50 individual state governments that make up the United States of America. It was drafted by John Adams, Samuel Adams, and James Bowdoin during the Massachusetts Constitutional Convention between September 1 and October 30, 1779. Following approval by town meetings, the Constitution was ratified on June 15, 1780, became effective on October 25, 1780, and remains the oldest functioning written constitution in continuous effect in the world.

The Massachusetts Constitution was the last of the first set of the state constitutions to be written. Consequently, it was more sophisticated than many of the other documents. Among the improvements was the structure of the document itself; instead of just a listing of provisions, it had a structure of chapters, sections, and articles. This structure was replicated by the U.S. Constitution. It also had substantial influence on the subsequent revisions of many of the other state constitutions. The Massachusetts Constitution has four parts: a preamble, a declaration of rights, a description of the framework of government, and articles of amendment.

The constitutional conventional pioneered by Massachusetts became a crucial component of the ratification process through which the United States Constitution was accepted by the states, including Massachusetts, in the 1780s.

The Document

Massachusetts Constitution

Preamble

The end of the institution, maintenance, and administration of government is to secure the existence of the body-politic, to protect it, and to furnish the individuals who compose it with the power of enjoying, in safety and tranquillity, their natural rights and the blessings of life; and

---

[7] [*] Originally published as "Massachusetts Constitution," *Wikipedia*, Wikimedia Foundation, Inc., San Francisco, California, November 2009. For additional information see "John Adams and the Massachusetts Constitution," *Education Resource Center Report*, Supreme Judicial Court, Commonwealth of Massachusetts, Boston, Massachusetts, 2007. This agency is listed in the *National Resource Directory* section of this volume.

whenever these great objects are not obtained the people have a right to alter the government, and to take measures necessary for their safety, prosperity, and happiness.

The body politic is formed by a voluntary association of individuals; it is a social compact by which the whole people covenants with each citizen and each citizen with the whole people that all shall be governed by certain laws for the common good. It is the duty of the people, therefore, in framing a constitution of government, to provide for an equitable mode of making laws, as well as for an impartial interpretation and a faithful execution of them; that every man may, at all times, find his security in them.

We, therefore, the people of Massachusetts, acknowledging, with grateful hearts, the goodness of the great Legislator of the universe, in affording us, in the course of His providence, an opportunity, deliberately and peaceably, without fraud, violence, or surprise, of entering into an original, explicit, and solemn compact with each other, and of forming a new constitution of civil government for ourselves and posterity; and devoutly imploring His direction in so interesting a design, do agree upon, ordain, and establish the following declaration of rights and frame of government as the constitution of the commonwealth of Massachusetts.

PART THE FIRST

A Declaration of the Rights of the Inhabitants of the Commonwealth of Massachusetts.

Article I. All men are born free and equal, and have certain natural, essential, and unalienable rights; among which may be reckoned the right of enjoying and defending their lives and liberties; that of acquiring, possessing, and protecting property; in fine, that of seeking and obtaining their safety and happiness.

Art. II. It is the right as well as the duty of all men in society, publicly and at stated seasons, to worship the Supreme Being, the great Creator and Preserver of the universe. And no subject shall be hurt, molested, or restrained, in his person, liberty, or estate, for worshipping God in the manner and season most agreeable to the dictates of his own conscience, or for his religious profession or sentiments, provided he doth not disturb the public peace or obstruct others in their religious worship.

Art. III. As the happiness of a people and the good order and preservation of civil government essentially depend upon piety, religion, and morality, and as these cannot be generally diffused through a community but by the institution of the public worship of God and of the public instructions in piety, religion, and morality: Therefore, To promote their happiness and to secure the good order and preservation of their government, the people of this commonwealth have a right to invest their legislature with power to authorize and require, and the legislature shall, from time to time, authorize and require, the several towns, parishes, precincts, and other bodies-politic or religious societies to make suitable provision, at their own expense, for the institution of the public worship of God and for the support and maintenance of public Protestant teachers of piety, religion, and morality in all cases where such provision shall not be made voluntarily.

And the people of this commonwealth have also a right to, and do, invest their legislature with authority to enjoin upon all the subject an attendance upon the instructions of the public teachers aforesaid, at stated times and seasons, if there be any on whose instructions they can conscientiously and conveniently attend.

Provided, notwithstanding, That the several towns, parishes, precincts, and other bodies-politic, or religious societies, shall at all times have the exclusive right and electing their public teachers and of contracting with them for their support and maintenance.

And all moneys paid by the subject to the support of public worship and of public teachers aforesaid shall, if he require it, be uniformly applied to the support of the public teacher or teachers of his own religious sect or denomination, provided there be any on whose instructions he attends; otherwise it may be paid toward the support of the teacher or teachers of the parish or precinct in which the said moneys are raised.

And every denomination of Christians, demeaning themselves peaceably and as good subjects of the commonwealth, shall be equally under the protection of the law; and no subordination of any sect or denomination to another shall ever be established by law.

Art. IV. The people of this commonwealth have the sole and exclusive right of governing themselves as a free, sovereign, and independent State, and do, and forever hereafter shall, exercise and enjoy every power, jurisdiction, and right which is not, or may not hereafter be, by them expressly delegated to the United States of America in Congress assembled.

Art. V. All power residing originally in the people, and being derived from them, the several magistrates and officers of government vested with authority, whether legislative, executive, or judicial, are the substitutes and agents, and are at all times accountable to them.

Art. VI. No man nor corporation or association of men have any other title to obtain advantages, or particular and exclusive privileges distinct from those of the community, than what rises from the consideration of services rendered to the public, and this title being in nature neither hereditary nor transmissible to children or descendants or relations by blood; the idea of a man born a magistrate, lawgiver, or judge is absurd and unnatural.

Art. VII. Government is instituted for the common good, for the protection, safety, prosperity, and happiness of the people, and not for the profit, honor, or private interest of any one man, family, or class of men; therefore the people alone have an incontestable, unalienable, and indefeasible right to institute government, and to reform, alter, or totally change the same when their protection, safety, prosperity, and happiness require it.

Art. VIII. In order to prevent those who are vested with authority from becoming oppressors, the people have a right at such periods and in such manner as they shall establish by their frame of government, to cause their public officers to return to private life; and to fill up vacant places by certain and regular elections and appointments.

Art. IX. All elections ought to be free; and all the inhabitants of this commonwealth, having such qualifications as they shall establish by their frame of government, have an equal right to elect officers, and to be elected, for public employments.

Art. X. Every individual of the society has a right to be protected by it in the enjoyment of his life, liberty, and property, according to standing laws. He is obliged, consequently, to contribute his share to expense of this protection; to give his personal service, or an equivalent, when necessary; but no part of the property of any individual can, with justice, be taken from him, or applied to public uses, without his own consent, or that of the representative body of the people. In fine, the people of this commonwealth are not controllable by any other laws than those to which their constitutional representative body have given their consent. And whenever the public exigencies require that the property of any individual should be appropriated to public uses, he shall receive a reasonable compensation therefor.

Art. XI. Every subject of the commonwealth ought to find a certain remedy, by having recourse to the laws, for all injuries or wrongs which he may receive in his person, property, or character. He ought to obtain right and justice freely, and without being obliged to purchase it; completely, and without any denial; promptly, and without delay, conformably to the laws.

Art. XII. No subject shall be held to answer for any crimes or no offence until the same if fully and plainly, substantially and formally, described to him; or be compelled to accuse, or furnish evidence against himself; and every subject shall have a right to produce all proofs that may be favorable to him; to meet the witnesses against him face to face, and to be fully heard in his defence by himself, or his counsel at his election. And no subject shall be arrested, imprisoned, despoiled, or deprived of his property, immunities, or privileges, put out of the protection of the law, exiled or deprived of his life, liberty, or estate, but by the judgment of his peers, or the law of the land.

And the legislature shall not make any law that shall subject any person to a capital or infamous punishment, excepting for the government of the army and navy, without trial by jury.

Art. XIII. In criminal prosecutions, the verification of facts, in the vicinity where they happen, is one of the greatest securities of the life, liberty, and property of the citizen.

Art. XIV. Every subject has a right to be secure from all unreasonable searches and seizures of his person, his houses, his papers, and all his possessions. All warrants, therefore, are contrary to this right, if the cause or foundation of them be not previously supported by oath or affirmation, and if the order in the warrant to a civil officer, to make search in suspected places, or to arrest one or more suspected persons, or to seize their property, be not accompanied with a special designation of the persons or objects of search, arrest, or seizure; and no warrant ought to be issued but in cases, and with the formalities, prescribed by the laws.

Art. XV. In all controversies concerning property, and in all suits between two or more persons, except in cases in which it has heretofore been otherways used and practised, the parties have a right to a trial by jury; and this method of procedure shall be held sacred, unless, in causes arising on the high seas, and such as relate to mariners' wages, the legislature shall hereafter find it necessary to alter it.

Art. XVI. The liberty of the press is essential to the security of freedom in a State; it ought not, therefore, to be restrained in this commonwealth.

Art. XVII. The people have a right to keep and to bear arms for the common defence. And as, in time of peace, armies are dangerous to liberty, they ought not to be maintained without the consent of the legislature; and the military power shall always be held in an exact subordination to the civil authority and be governed by it.

Art. XVIII. A frequent recurrence to the fundamental principles of the constitution, and a constant adherence to those of piety, justice, moderation, temperance, industry, and frugality, are absolutely necessary to preserve the advantages of liberty and to maintain a free government. The people ought, consequently, to have a particular attention to all those principles, in the choice of their officers and representatives; and they have a right to require of their lawgivers and magistrates an exact and constant observation of them, in the formation and execution of the laws necessary for the good administration of the commonwealth.

Art. XIX. The people have a right, in an orderly and peaceable manner, to assemble to consult upon the common good; give instructions to their representatives, and to request of the legislative body, by the way of addresses, petitions, or remonstrances, redress of the wrongs done them, and of the grievances they suffer.

Art. XX. The power of suspending the laws, or the execution of the laws, ought never to be exercised but by the legislature, or by authority derived from it, to be exercised in such particular cases only as the legislature shall expressly provide for.

Art. XXI. The freedom of deliberation, speech, and debate, in either house of the legislature, is so essential to the rights of the people, that it cannot be the foundation of any accusation or prosecution, action or complaint, in any other court of place whatsoever.

Art. XXII. The legislature ought frequently to assemble for address of grievances, for correcting, strengthening, and confirming the laws, and for making new laws, as the common good may require.

Art. XXIII. No subsidy, charge, tax, impost, or duties, ought to be established, fixed, laid, or levied, under any pretext whatsoever, without the consent of the people, or their representatives in the legislature.

Art. XXIV. Laws made to punish for actions done before the existence of such laws, and which have not been declared crimes by preceding laws, are unjust, oppressive, and inconsistent with the fundamental principles of a free government.

Art. XXV. No subject ought, in any case, or in any time, to be declared guilty of treason or felony by the legislature.

Art. XXVI. No magistrate or court of law shall demand excessive bail or sureties, impose excessive fines, or inflict cruel or unusual punishments.

Art. XXVII. In time of peace, no soldier ought to be quartered in any house without the consent of the owner; and in time of war, such quarters ought not be made but by the civil magistrate, in a manner ordained by the legislature.

Art. XXVIII. No person can in any case be subjected to law-martial, or to any penalties or pains, by virtue of that law, except those employed in the army or navy, and except the militia in actual service, but by authority of the legislature.

Art. XXIX. It is essential to the preservation of the rights of every individual, his life, liberty, property, and character, that there be an impartial interpretation of the laws, and administration of justice. It is the right of every citizen to be tried by judges as free, impartial, and independent as the lot of humanity will admit. It is, therefore, not only the best policy, but for the security of the rights of the people, and of every citizen, that the judges of the supreme judicial court should hold their offices as long as they behave themselves well, and that they should have honorable salaries ascertained and established by standing laws.

Art. XXX. In the government of this commonwealth, the legislative department shall never exercise the executive and judicial powers, or either of them; the executive shall never exercise the legislative and judicial powers, or either of them; the judicial shall never exercise the legislative and executive powers, or either of them; to the end it may be a government of laws, and not of men.

PART THE SECOND

The Frame of Government

The people inhabiting the territory formerly called the province of Massachusetts Bay do hereby solemnly and mutually agree with each other to form themselves into a free, sovereign, and independent body-politic or State, by the name of the commonwealth of Massachusetts.

CHAPTER I. – THE LEGISLATIVE POWER

Section I. – The General Court

Article I. The department of legislation shall be formed by two branches, a senate and house of representatives; each of which shall have a negative on the other.

The legislative body shall assemble every year on the last Wednesday in May, and at such other times as they shall judge necessary; and shall dissolve and be dissolved on the day next preceding the said last Wednesday in May; and shall be styled the *General Court of Massachusetts.*

Art. II. No bill or resolve of the senate or house of representatives shall become a law, and have force as such, until it shall have been laid before the governor for his revisal; and if he, upon such revision, approve thereof, he shall signify his approbation by signing the same. But if he have any objection to the passing such bill or resolve, he shall return the same, together with his objections thereto, in writing, to the senate or house of representatives, in whichsoever the same shall have originated, who shall enter the objections sent down by the governor, at large, on their records, and proceed to reconsider the said bill or resolve; but if, after such reconsideration, two-thirds of the said senate or house of representatives shall, notwithstanding the said objections, agree to pass the same, it shall, together with the objections, be sent to the other branch of the legislature, where it shall also be reconsidered, and if approved by two-thirds of the members present, shall have the force of law; but in all such cases, the vote of both houses shall be determined by yeas and nays; and the names of the persons voting for or against the said bill or resolve shall be entered upon the public records of the commonwealth.

And in order to prevent unnecessary delays, if any bill or resolve shall not be returned by the governor within five days after it shall have been presented, the same shall have the force of law.

Art. III. The general court shall forever have full power and authority to erect and constitute judicatories and courts of record or other courts, to be held in the name of the commonwealth, for the hearing, trying, and determining of all manner of crimes, offences, pleas, processes, plaints, actions, matters, causes, and things whatsoever, arising or happening within the commonwealth, or between or concerning persons inhabiting or residing, or brought within the same; whether the same be criminal or civil, or whether the said crimes be capital or not capital, and whether the said pleas be real, personal, or mixed; and for the awarding and making out of execution thereupon; to which courts and judicatories are hereby given and granted full power and authority, from time to time, to administer oaths or affirmations, for the better discovery of truth in any matter in controversy, or depending before them.

Art. IV. And further, full power and authority are hereby given and granted to the said general court from time to time, to make, ordain, and establish all manner of wholesome and reasonable orders, laws, statutes, and ordinances, directions and instructions, either with penalties or without, so as the same be not repugnant or contrary to this constitution, as they shall judge to be for the good and welfare of this commonwealth, and for the government and ordering thereof, and of the subjects of the same, and for the necessary support and defence of the government thereof; and to name and settle annually, or provide by fixed laws, for the naming and settling all civil officers within the said commonwealth, the election, and constitution of whom are not hereafter in this form of government otherwise provided for; and to set forth the several duties, powers, and limits of the several civil and military officers of this commonwealth, and the forms of such oaths or affirmations as shall be respectively administered unto them for the execution of their several offices and places, so as the same be not repugnant or contrary to this constitution; and to impose and levy proportional and reasonable assessments, rates, and taxes, upon all the inhabitants of, and persons resident, and estates lying, within the said commonwealth; and also to impose and levy reasonable duties and excises upon any produce, goods, wares, merchandise, and commodities whatsoever, brought into, produced, manufactured, or being within the same; to be issued and disposed of by warrant, under the hand of the governor of this commonwealth, for the time being, with the advice and consent of the council, for the public service, in the necessary defence and support of the government of the said commonwealth, and the protection and preservation of the subjects thereof, according to such acts as are or shall be in force within the same.

And while the public charges of government, or any part thereof, shall be assessed on polls and estates, in the manner that has hitherto been practised, in order that such assessments may be made with equality, there shall be a valuation of estates within the commonwealth, taken anew once in every ten years at least, and as much oftener as the general court shall order.

CHAPTER I

Section 2.– Senate

Article I. There shall be annually elected, by the freeholders and other inhabitants of this commonwealth, qualified as in this constitution is provided, forty persons to be councillors and senators, for the year ensuing their election; to be chosen by the inhabitants of the districts into which the commonwealth may from time to time be divided by the general court for that purpose; and the general court, in assigning the numbers to be elected by the respective districts, shall govern themselves by the proportion of the public taxes paid by the said districts; and timely make known to the inhabitants of the commonwealth the limits of each district, and the number of councillors and senators to be chosen therein: *Provided*, That the number of such districts shall never be less than thirteen; and that no district be so large as to entitle the same to choose more than six senators.

And the several counties in this commonwealth shall, until the general court shall determine it necessary to alter the said districts, be districts for the choice of councillors and senators, (except that the counties of Dukes County and Nantucket shall form one district for that purpose,) and shall elect the following number for councillors and senators, viz: ... [39 senators].

Art. II. The senate shall be the first branch of the legislature; and the senators shall be chosen in the following manner, viz: There shall be a meeting on the first Monday in April, annually, forever, of the inhabitants of each town in the several counties of this commonwealth, to be called by the selectmen, and warned in due course of law, at least seven days before the first Monday in April, for the purpose of electing persons to be senators and councillors; and at such meetings every male inhabitant of twenty-one year of age and upwards, having a freehold estate of the value of sixty pounds, shall have a right to give in his vote for the senators for the district of which he is an inhabitant. And to remove all doubts concerning the meaning of the word "inhabitant," in this constitution, every person shall be considered as an inhabitant, for the purpose of electing and being elected into any office or place within this State, in that town, district, or plantation where he dwelleth or hath his home.

The selectmen of the several towns shall preside at such meetings impartially, and shall receive the votes of all the inhabitants of such towns, present and qualified to vote for senators, and shall sort and count them in open town meeting, and in presence of the town clerk, who shall make a fair record, in presence of the selectmen, and in open town meeting, of the name of every person voted for, and of the number of votes against his name; and a fair copy of this record shall be attested by the selectmen and the town clerk, and shall be sealed up, directed to the secretary of the commonwealth, for the time being, with a superscription expressing the purport of the contents thereof, and delivered by the town clerk of such towns to the sheriff of the county in which such town lies, thirty days at least before the last Wednesday in May, annually; or it shall be delivered into the secretary's office seventeen days at least before the said last Wednesday in May; and the sheriff of each county shall deliver all such certificates, by him received, into the secretary's office seventeen days before the said last Wednesday in May.

And the inhabitants of the plantations unincorporated, qualified as this constitution provides, who are or shall be empowered and required to assess taxes upon themselves toward the support of government, shall have the same privilege of voting for councillors and senators, in the plantations where they reside, as town inhabitants have in their respective towns; and the plantation meetings for that purpose shall be held annually, on the same first Monday in April, at such place in the plantations, respectively, as the assessors thereof shall direct; which assessors shall have like authority for notifying the electors, collecting and returning the votes, as the selectmen and town clerks have in their several towns by this constitution. And all other persons living in places unincorporated, (qualified as aforesaid,) who shall be assessed to the support of government by assessors of an adjacent town, shall have the privilege of giving in their votes for councillors and senators in the town where they shall be assessed, and be notified of the place of meeting by the selectmen of the town where they shall be assessed, for that purpose, accordingly.

Art. III. And that there may be a due convention of senators, on the last Wednesday in May, annually, the governor, with five of the council, for the time being, shall, as soon as may be, examine the returned copies of such records; and fourteen days before the said day he shall issue his summons to such persons as shall appear to be chosen by a majority of voters to attend on that day, and take their seats accordingly: *Provided, nevertheless,* That for the first year the said returned copies shall be examined by the president and five of the council of the former constitution of government; and the said president shall, in like manner, issue his summons to the persons so elected, that they may take their seats as aforesaid.

Art. IV. The senate shall be the final judge of the elections, returns, and qualifications of their own members, as pointed out in the constitution; and shall, on the said last Wednesday in May, annually, determine and declare who are elected by each district to be senators by a majority of votes; and in case there shall not be the full number of senators returned, elected by a majority of votes for any district, the deficiency shall be supplied in the following manner, viz: The members of the house of representatives, and such senators as shall be declared elected, shall take the names of such persons as shall be found to have the highest number of votes in such district, and not elected, amounting to twice the number of senators wanting, if there be so many voted for, and out of these shall elect by ballot a number of senators sufficient to fill up the vacancies in such district; and in this manner all such vacancies shall be filled up in every district of the commonwealth; and in like manner all vacancies in the senate, arising by death, removal out of the State or otherwise, shall be supplied as soon as may after such vacancies shall happen.

Art. V. *Provided, nevertheless,* That no person shall be capable of being elected as a senator [who is not seized in his own right of a freehold within this commonwealth, of the value of three hundred pounds at least, or possessed of personal estate to the value of six hundred pounds at least, or of both to the amount of the same sum, and] who has not been an inhabitant of this commonwealth for the space of five years immediately preceding his election, and, at the time of his election, he shall be an inhabitant in the district for which he shall be chosen.

Art. VI. The senate shall have power to adjourn themselves; provided such adjournments do not exceed two days at a time.

Art. VII. The senate shall choose its own president, appoint its own officers, and determine its own rules of proceedings.

Art. VIII. The senate shall be a court, with full authority to hear and determine all impeachments made by the house of representatives, against any officer or officers of the commonwealth, for misconduct and maladministration in their offices; but, previous to the trial of every impeachment, the members of the senate shall, respectively, be sworn truly and impartially to try and determine the charge in question, according to the evidence. Their judgment, however, shall not extend further than to removal from office, and disqualification to hold or enjoy any place of honor, trust, or profit under this commonwealth; but the part so convicted shall be, nevertheless, liable to indictment, trial, judgment, and punishment, according to the laws of the land.

Art. IX. Not less than sixteen members of the senate shall constitute a quorum for doing business.

Chapter I.

Section 3. – House of Representatives

Article I. There shall be, in the legislature of this commonwealth, a representation of the people, annually elected, and founded upon the principle of equality.

Art. II. And in order to provide for a representation of the citizens of this commonwealth, founded upon the principle of equality, every corporate town containing one hundred and fifty ratable polls, may elect one representative; every corporate town containing three hundred and seventy-five ratable polls, may elect two representatives; every corporate town containing six hundred ratable polls, may elect three representatives; and proceeding in that manner, making two hundred and twenty-five ratable polls the mean increasing number for every additional representative.

Provided, nevertheless, That each town now incorporated, not having one hundred and fifty ratable polls, may elect one representative; but no place shall hereafter be incorporated with the privilege of electing a representative, unless there are within the same one hundred and fifty ratable polls.

And the house of representatives shall have power, from time to time, to impose fines upon such towns as shall neglect to choose and return members of the same, agreeably to this constitution.

The expenses of travelling to the general assembly and returning home, once in every session, and no more, shall be paid by the government out of the public treasury, to every member who shall attend as seasonably as he can, in the judgment of the house, and does not depart without leave.

Art. III. Every member of the house of representatives shall be chosen by written votes; and, for one year at least next preceding his election, shall have been an inhabitant of, and have been seized in his own right of a freehold of the value of one hundred pounds, within the town he shall be chosen to represent, or any ratable estate to the value of two hundred pounds; and he shall cease to represent the said town immediately on his ceasing to be qualified as aforesaid.

Art. IV. Every male person being twenty-one years of age, and resident in any particular town in this commonwealth, for the space of one year next preceding, having a freehold estate within the same town, of the annual income of three pounds, or any estate of the value of sixty pounds, shall have a right to vote in the choice of a representative or representatives for the said town.

Art. V. The members of the house of representatives shall be chosen annually in the month of May, ten days at least before the last Wednesday of that month.

Art. VI. The house of representatives shall be the grand inquest of this commonwealth; and all impeachments made by them shall be heard and tried by the senate.

Art. VII. All money bills shall originate in the house of representatives; but the senate may propose or concur with amendments, as on other bills.

Art. VIII. The house of representatives shall have power to adjourn themselves; provided such adjournments shall not exceed two days at a time.

Art. IX. Not less than sixty members of the house of representatives shall constitute a quorum for doing business.

Art. X. The house of representatives shall be the judge of the returns, elections, and qualifications of its own members, as point out in the constitution; shall choose their own speaker, appoint their own officers, and settle the rules and order of proceeding in their own house. They shall have authority to punish by imprisonment every person, not a member, who shall be guilty of disrespect to the house, by any disorderly or contemptuous behavior in its presence; or who, in the town where the general court is sitting, and during the time of its sitting, shall threaten harm to the body or estate of any of its members, for anything said or done in the house; or who shall assault any of them therefor; or who shall assault or arrest any witness, or other person, ordered to attend the house, in his way in going or returning; or who shall rescue any person arrested by the order of the house.

And no member of the house of representatives shall be arrested, or held to bail on mesne process, during his going unto, returning from, or his attending the general assembly.

Art. XI. The senate shall have the same powers in the like cases; and the governor and council shall have the same authority to punish in like cases; *Provided*, That no imprisonment, on the warrant or order of the governor, council, senate, or house of representatives, for either of the above-described offences, be for a term exceeding thirty days.

And the senate and house of representatives may try and determine all cases where their rights and privileges are concerned, and which, by the constitution, they have authority to try and determine, by committees of their own members, or in such other way as they may, respectively, think best.

Chapter II. – Executive Power

Section I. – Governor

Article I. There shall be a supreme executive magistrate, who shall be styled "The governor of the commonwealth of Massachusetts;" and whose title shall be "His Excellency."

Art. II. The governor shall be chosen annually; and no person shall be eligible to this office, unless, at the time of his election, he shall have been an inhabitant of this commonwealth for seven years next preceding; and unless he shall, at the same time, be seized, in his own right, of a freehold, within the commonwealth, of the value of one thousand pounds; and unless he shall declare himself to be of the Christian religion.

Art. III. Those persons who shall be qualified to vote for senators and representatives, within the several towns of this commonwealth, shall, at a meeting to be called for that purpose, on the first Monday of April, annually, give in their votes for a governor to the selectmen, who shall preside at such meetings; and the town clerk, in the presence and with the assistance of the selectmen, shall, in open town meeting, sort and count the votes, and form a list of the persons voted for, with the number of votes for each person against his name; and shall make a fair record of the same in the town books, and a public declaration thereof in the said meeting; and shall, in the presence of the inhabitants, seal up copies of the said list, attested by him and the selectmen, and transmit the same to the sheriff of the county, thirty days at least before the last Wednesday in May; and the sheriff shall transmit the same to the secretary's office, seventeen days at least before the said last Wednesday in May; or the selectmen may cause returns of the same to be made, to the office of the secretary of the commonwealth, seventeen days at least before the said day; and the secretary shall lay the same before the senate and the house of representatives, on the last Wednesday in May, to be by them examined; and in case of an election by a majority of all the votes returned, the choice shall be by them declared and published; but if no person shall have a majority of votes, the house of representatives shall, by ballot, elect two out of four persons, who had the highest number of votes, if so many shall have been voted for; but, if otherwise, out of the number voted for; and make return to the senate of the two persons so elected; on which the senate shall proceed, by ballot, to elect one, who shall be declared governor.

Art. IV. The governor shall authority, from time to time, at his discretion, to assemble and call together the councillors of this commonwealth for the time being; and the governor, with the said councillors, or five of them at least, shall and may, from time to time, hold and keep a council, for the ordering and directing the affairs of the commonwealth, agreeably to the constitution and the laws of the land.

Art. V. The governor, with advice of council, shall have full power and authority, during the session of the general court, to adjourn or prorogue the same at any time the two houses shall desire; and to dissolve the same on the day next preceding the last Wednesday in May; and, in the recess of the said court, to prorogue the same from time to time, not exceeding ninety days in any one recess; and to call it together sooner than the time to which it may be adjourned or prorogued, if the welfare of the commonwealth shall require the same; and in case of any infectious distemper prevailing in the place where the said court is next at any time to convene, or any other cause happening, whereby danger may arise to the health or lives of the members from their attendance, he may direct the session to be held at some other the most convenient place within the State.

And the governor shall dissolve the said general court on the day next preceding the last Wednesday in May.

Art. VI. In cases of disagreement between the two houses, with regard to the necessity, expediency, or time of adjournment or prorogation, the governor, with advice of the council, shall have a right to adjourn or prorogue the general court, not exceeding ninety days, as he shall determine the public good shall require.

Art. VII. The governor of this commonwealth, for the time being, shall be the commander-in-chief of the army and navy, and of all the military forces of the State, by sea and land; and shall have full power, by himself or by any commander, or other officer or officers, from time to time, to train, instruct, exercise, and govern the militia and navy; and, for the special defence and safety of the commonwealth, to assemble in martial array, and put in warlike posture, the inhabitants thereof, and to lead and conduct them, and with them to encounter, repel, resist, expel, and pursue, by force of arms, as by sea as by land, within or within the limits of this commonwealth; and also to kill, slay, and destroy, if necessary, and conquer, by all fitting ways, enterprises, and means whatsoever, all and every such person and persons as shall, at any time hereafter, in a hostile manner, attempt or enterprise the destruction, invasion, detriment, or annoyance of this commonwealth; and to use and exercise over the army and navy, and over the militia in actual service, the law-martial, in time of war or invasion, and also in time of rebellion, declared by the legislature to exist, as occasion shall necessarily require; and to take and surprise, by all ways and means whatsoever, all and every such person or persons, with their ships, arms, and ammunition, and other goods, as shall, in a hostile manner, invade, or attempt the invading, conquering, or annoying this commonwealth; and that the governor be intrusted with all these and other powers incident to the offices of captain-general and commander-in-chief, and admiral, to be exercised agreeably to the rules and regulations of the constitution and the laws of the land, and not otherwise.

Provided, That the said governor shall not, at any time hereafter, by virtue of any power by this constitution granted, or hereafter to be granted to him by the legislature, transport any of the inhabitants of this commonwealth, or oblige them to march out of the limits of the same, without their free and voluntary consent, or the consent of the general court; except so far as may be necessary to march or transport them by land or water for the defence of such part of the State to which they cannot otherwise conveniently have access.

Art. VIII. The power of pardoning offences, except such as persons may be convicted of before the senate, by an impeachment of the house, shall be in the governor, by and with the advice of council; but no charter or pardon, granted by the governor, with the advice of the council, before conviction, shall avail the party pleading the same, notwithstanding any general or particular expressions contained therein, descriptive of the offence or offences intended to be pardoned.

Art. IX. All judicial officers, the attorney-general, the solicitor-general, all sheriffs, coroners, and registers of probate, shall be nominated and appointed by the governor, by and with the advice and consent of the council; and every such nomination shall be made by the governor, and made at least seven days prior to such appointment.

Art. X. The captains and subalterns of the militia shall be elected by the written votes of the train-band and alarm-list of their respective companies, of twenty years of age and upwards; the field-officers of regiments shall be elected by the written votes of the captains and subalterns of their respective regiments; the brigadiers shall be elected, in like manner, by the field-officers of their respective brigades; and such officers, so elected, shall be commissioned by the governor, who shall determine their rank.

The legislature shall, by standing laws, direct the time and manner of convening the electors, and of collecting votes, and of certifying to the governer the officers elected.

The major-generals shall be appointed by the senate and house of representatives, each having a negative upon the other; and be commissioned by the governor.

And if the electors of brigadiers, field-officers, captains, or subalterns shall neglect or refuse to make such elections, after being duly notified, according to the laws for the time being, then the governor, with the advice of council, shall appoint suitable persons to fill such offices.

And no officer, duly commissioned to command in the militia, shall be removed from his office, but by the address of both houses to the governor, or by fair trial in court-martial, pursuant to the laws of the commonwealth for the time being.

The commanding officers of regiments shall appoint their adjutants and quartermasters; the brigadiers, their brigade-majors; and the major-generals, their aids; and the governor shall appoint the adjutant-general.

The governor, with the advice of council, shall appoint all officers of the Continental Army, whom, by the Confederation of the United States, it is provided that this commonwealth shall appoint, as also all officers of forts and garrisons.

The divisions of the militia into brigades, regiments, and companies, made in pursuance of the militia-laws now in force, shall be considered as the proper divisions of the militia in this commonwealth, until the same shall be altered in pursuance of some future law.

Art. XI. No moneys shall be issued out of the treasury of this commonwealth and disposed of, except such sums as may be appropriated for the redemption of bills of credit or treasurer's notes, or for the payment of interest arising thereon, but by warrant under the hand of the governor for the time being, with the advice and consent of the council for the necessary defence and support of the commonwealth, and for the protection and preservation of the inhabitants thereof, agreeably to the acts and resolves of the general court.

Art. XII. All public boards, the commissary-general, all superintending officers of public magazines and stores, belonging to this commonwealth, and all commanding officers of forts and garrisons within the same, shall, once in every three months, officially and without requisition, and at other times, when required by the governor, deliver to him an account of all goods, stores, provisions, ammunition, cannon, with their appendages, and small-arms with their accoutrements, and of all other public property whatever under their care, respectively; distinguishing the quantity, number, quality, and kind of each, as particularly as may be; together with the condition of such forts and garrisons; and the said commanding officer shall exhibit to the governor, when required by him, true and exact plans of such forts, and of the land and sea, or harbor or harbors, adjacent.

And the said boards, and all public officers, shall communicate to the governor, as soon as may be after receiving the same, all letters, dispatches, and intelligences of a public nature, which shall be directed to them respectively.

Art. XIII. As the public good requires that the governor should not be under the undue influence of any of the members of the general court, by a dependence on them for his support; that he should, in all cases, act with freedom for the benefit of the public; that he should not have his attention necessarily diverted from that object to his private concerns; and that he should maintain the dignity of the commonwealth in the character of its chief magistrate, it is necessary that he should have an honorable stated salary, of a fixed and permanent value, amply sufficient for those purposes, and established by standing laws; and it shall be among the first acts of the general court, after the commencement of this constitution, to establish such salary by law accordingly.

Permanent and honorable salaries shall also be established by law for the justices of the supreme judicial court.

And if it shall be found that any of the salaries aforesaid, so established, are insufficient, they shall, from time to time, be enlarged, as the general court shall judge proper.

CHAPTER II.

Section 2. – Lieutenant-Governor

Article I. There shall be annually elected a lieutenant-governor of the commonwealth of Massachusetts, whose title shall be "His Honor;" and who shall be qualified, in point of religion, property, and residence in the commonwealth, in the same manner with the governor; and the day and manner of his election, and the qualification of the electors, shall be the same as are required in the election of a governor. The return of the votes for this officer, and the declaration of his election, shall be in the same manner; and if no one person shall be found to have a majority of all the votes returned, the vacancy shall be filled by the senate and house of representatives, in the same manner as the governor is to be elected, in case no one person shall have a majority of the votes of the people to be governor.

Art. II. The governor, and in his absence the lieutenant-governor, shall be president of the council; but shall have no voice in council; and the lieutenant-governor shall always be a member of the council, except when the chair of the governor shall be vacant.

Art. III. Whenever the chair of the governor shall be vacant, by reason of his death, or absence from the commonwealth, or otherwise, the lieutenant-governor, for the time being, shall, during such vacancy perform all the duties incumbent upon the governor, and shall have and exercise all the powers and authorities which, by this constitution, the governor is vested with, when personally present.

CHAPTER II.

Section 3. – Council, and the Manner of Settling Elections by the Legislature

Article I. There shall be a council, for advising the governor in the executive part of the government, to consist of nine persons besides the lieutenant-governor, whom the governor, for the time being, shall have full power and authority, from time to time, at this discretion, to assemble and call together; and the governor, with the said councillors, or five of them at least, shall and may, from time to time, hold and keep a council, for the ordering and directing the affairs of the commonwealth, according to the laws of the land.

Art. II. Nine councillors shall be annually chosen from among the persons returned for councillors and senators, on the last Wednesday in May, by the joint ballot of the senators and representatives assembled in one room; and in case there shall not be found, upon the first choice, the whole number of nine persons who will accept a seat in the council, the deficiency shall be made up by the electors aforesaid from among the people at large; and the number of senators left shall constitute the senate for the year. The seats of the persons thus elected from the senate, and accepting the trust, shall be vacated in the senate.

Art. III. The councillors, in the civil arrangements of the commonwealth, shall have rank next after the lieutenant-governor.

Art. IV. Not more than two councillors shall be chosen out of any one district in this commonwealth.

Art. V. The resolutions and advice of the council shall be recorded in a register and signed by the members present; and this record may be called for, at any time, by either house of the legislature; and any member of the council may insert his opinion, contrary to the resolution of the majority.

Art. VI. Whenever the office of the governor and lieutenant-governor shall be vacant by reason of death, absence, or otherwise, then the council, or the major part of them, shall, during such vacancy, have full power and authority to do and execute all and every such acts, matters, and things, as the governor or the lieutenant-governor might or could, by virtue of this constitution, do or execute, if they, or either of them, were personally present.

Art. VII. And whereas the elections appointed to be made by this constitution on the last Wednesday in May annually, by the two houses of the legislature, may not be completed on that day, the said elections may be adjourned from day to day, until the same shall be completed. And the order of elections shall be as follows: The vacancies in the senate, if any, shall first be filled up; the governor and lieutenant-governor shall then be elected, provided there should be no choice of them by the people; and afterwards the two houses shall proceed to the election of the council.

CHAPTER II.

Section 4. – Secretary, Treasurer, Commissary, etc.

Article I. The secretary, treasurer, and receiver-general, and the commissary-general, notaries public, and naval officers, shall be chosen annually, by joint ballot of the senators and representatives, in one room. And, that the citizens of this commonwealth may be assured, from time to time, that the moneys remaining in the public treasury, upon the settlement and liquidation of the public accounts, are their property, no man shall be eligible as treasurer and receiver-general more than five years successively.

Art. II. The records of the commonwealth shall be kept in the office of the secretary, who may appoint his deputies, for whose conduct he shall be accountable; and he shall attend the governor and council, the senate and house of representatives in person or by his deputies, as they shall respectively require.

CHAPTER III.

Judiciary Power.

Article I. The tenure that all commission officers shall by law have in their offices shall be expressed in their respective commissions. All judicial officers, duly appointed, commissioned, and sworn, shall hold their offices during good behavior, excepting such concerning whom there is different provision made in this constitution: *Provided, nevertheless,* The governor, with consent of the council, may remove them upon the address of both houses of the legislature.

Art. II. Each branch of the legislature, as well as the governor and council, shall have authority to require the opinions of the justices of the supreme judicial court upon important questions of law, and upon solemn occasions.

Art. III. In order that the people may not suffer from the long continuance in place of any justice of the peace, who shall fail of discharging the important duties of his office with ability or fidelity, all commissions of justices of the peace shall expire and become void in the term of seven years from their respective dates; and, upon the expiration of any commission, the same may, if necessary, be renewed, or another person appointed, as shall most conduce to the well-being of the commonwealth.

Art. IV. The judges of probate of wills, and for granting letters of administration, shall hold their courts at such place or places, on fixed days, as the convenience of the people shall require; and the legislature shall, from time to time, hereafter, appoint such times and places; until which appointments the said courts shall be holden at the times and places which the respective judges shall direct.

Art. V. All causes of marriage, divorce, and alimony, and all appeals from the judges of probate, shall be heard and determined by the governor and council until the legislature shall, by law, make other provision.

CHAPTER IV.

Delegates to Congress

The delegates of this commonwealth to the Congress of the United States shall, some time in the month of June, annually, be elected by the joint ballot of the senate and house of representatives assembled together in one room; to serve in Congress for one year, to commence on the first Monday in November, then next ensuing. They shall have commissions under the hand of the governor, and the great seal of the commonwealth; but may be recalled at any time within the year, and others chosen and commissioned, in the same manner, in their stead.

CHAPTER V. – THE UNIVERSITY AT CAMBRIDGE, AND ENCOURAGEMENT OF LITERATURE, ETC.

Section 1. – The University

Article I. Whereas our wise and pious ancestors, so early as the year [1636], laid the foundation of Harvard College, in which university many persons of great prominence have, by the blessing of God, been initiated in those arts and sciences which qualified them for the public employments, both in church and State; and whereas the encouragement of arts and sciences, and all good literature, tends to the honor of God, the advantage of the Christian religion, and the great benefit of this and the other United States of America, it is declared, that the president and fellows of Harvard College, in their corporate capacity, and their successors in that capacity, their officers and servants, shall have, hold, use, exercise, and enjoy all the powers, authorities, rights, liberties, privileges, immunities, and franchises which they now have, or are entitled to have, hold, use, exercise, and enjoy; and the same are hereby ratified and confirmed unto them, the said president and fellows of Harvard College, and to their successors, and to their officers and servants, respectively, forever.

Art. II. And whereas there have been, at sundry times, by divers persons, gifts, grants, devises of houses, lands, tenements, goods, chattels, legacies, and conveyances heretofore made, either to Harvard College in Cambridge, in New England, or to the president and fellows of Harvard College, or to the said college, by some other description, under several charters successively, it is declared, that all the said gifts, grants, devises, legacies, and conveyances are hereby forever confirmed unto the president and fellows of Harvard College, and to their successors, in the capacity aforesaid, according to the true intent and meaning of the donor or donors, grantor or grantors, devisor or devisors.

Art. III. And whereas by an act of the general court of the colony of Massachusetts Bay, passed in the year [1642], the governor and deputy governor for the time being, and all the magistrates of that jurisdiction, were, with the President, and a number of the clergy, is the said act described, constituted the overseers of Harvard College; and it being necessary, in this new constitution of government, to ascertain who shall be deemed successors to the said governor, deputy governor, and magistrates, it is declared that the governor, lieutenant-governor, council, and senate of this commonwealth are, and shall be deemed, their successors; who, with the president of Harvard College, for the time being, together with the ministers of the congregational churches in the towns of Cambridge, Watertown, Charlestown, Boston, Roxbury and Dorchester, mentioned in the said act, shall be, and hereby are, vested with all the powers and authority belonging, or in any way appertaining, to the overseers of Harvard College: *Provided*, that nothing herein shall be construed to prevent the legislature of this commonwealth from making such alterations in the government of the said university as shall be conducive to its advantage, and the interest of the republic of letters, in as full a manner as might have been done by the legislature of the late province of the Massachusetts Bay.

CHAPTER V.

Section 2. – *The Encouragement of Literature, etc.*

Wisdom and knowledge, as well as virtue, diffused generally among the body of the people, being necessary for the preservation of their rights and liberties; and as these depend on spreading the opportunities and advantages of education in the various parts of the country, and among the different orders of the people, it shall be the duty of legislatures and magistrates, in all future periods of this commonwealth, to cherish the interests of literature and the sciences, and all seminaries of them; especially the university at Cambridge, public schools, and grammar-schools in the towns; to encourage private societies and public institutions, rewards and immunities, for the promotion of agriculture, arts, sciences, commerce, trades, manufactures, and a natural history of the country; to countenance and inculcate the principles of humanity and general benevolence, public and private charity, industry and frugality, honesty and punctuality in their dealings; sincerity, and good humor, and all social affections and generous sentiments, among the people.

CHAPTER VI.

Oaths and Subscriptions; Incompatibility of and Exclusion from Offices; Pecuniary Qualifications; Commissions; Writs; Confirmation of Laws; Habeas Corpus; The Enacting Style; Continuance of Officers; Provision for a Future Revisal of the Constitution, etc.

Article I. Any person chosen governor, lieutenant-governor, councillor, senator, or representative, and accepting the trust, shall, before he proceed to execute the duties of his place or office, make and subscribe the following declaration, viz:

"I, A.B., do declare that I believe the Christian religion, and have a firm persuasion of its truth; and that I am seized and possessed, in my own right, of the property required by the constitution, as one qualification for the office or place to which I am elected."

And the governor, lieutenant-governor, and councillors shall make and subscribe the said declaration, in the presence of the two houses of assembly; and the senators and representatives, first elected under this constitution, before the president and five of the council of the former constitution; and forever afterwards, before the governor and council for the time being. And every person chosen to either of the places or offices aforesaid, as also any persons appointed or commissioned to any judicial, executive, military, or other office under the government, shall, before he enters on the discharge of the business of his place or office, take and subscribe the following declaration and oaths or affirmations, viz:

"I, A.B., do truly and sincerely acknowledge, profess, testify, and declare that the commonwealth of Massachusetts is, and of right ought to be, a free, sovereign, and independent State, and I do swear that I will bear true faith and allegiance to the said commonwealth, and that I will defend the same against traitorous conspiracies and all hostile attempts whatsoever; and that I do renounce and abjure all allegiance, subjection, and obedience to the King, Queen, or government of Great Britain, (as the case may be,) and every other foreign power whatsoever; and that no foreign prince, person, prelate, state, or potentate hath, or ought to have, any jurisdiction, superiority, preeminence, authority, dispensing or other power, in any matter, civil, ecclesiastical, or spiritual, within this commonwealth; except the authority and power which is or may be vested by their constituents in the Congress of the United States; and I do further testify and declare that no man, or body of men, have, or can have, any right to absolve or discharge me from the obligation of this oath, declaration, or affirmation; and that I do make this acknowledgment, profession, testimony, declaration, denial, renunciation, and abjuration heartily and truly, according to the common meaning and acceptation of the foregoing words, without any equivocation, mental evasion, or secret reservation whatsoever: So help me, God."

"I, A.B., do solemnly swear and affirm that I will faithfully and impartially discharge and perform all the duties incumbent on me as _____, according to the best of my abilities and understanding, agreeably to the rules and regulations of the constitution and the laws of the commonwealth: So help me, God."

Provided always, That when any person, chosen and appointed as aforesaid, shall be of the denomination of people called Quakers, and shall decline taking the said oaths, he shall make his affirmation in the foregoing form, and subscribe the same, omitting the words, "I do swear," "and abjure," "oath or," "and abjuration," in the first oath; and in the second oath, the words, "swear and," and in each of them the words, "So help me, God;" subjoining instead thereof, "This I do under the pains and penalties of perjury."

And the said oaths or affirmations shall be taken and subscribed by the governor, lieutenant-governor, and councillors, before the president of the senate, in the presence of the two houses of assembly; and by the senators and representatives first elected under this constitution, before the president and five of the council of the former constitution; and forever afterwards before the governor and council for the time being; and by the residue of the officers aforesaid, before such persons and in such manner as from time to time shall be prescribed by the legislature.

Art. II. No governor, lieutenant-governor, or judge of the supreme judicial court shall hold any other office or place, under the authority of this commonwealth, except such as by the constitution they are admitted to hold, saving that the judges of the said court may hold the office of the justices of the peace through the State; nor shall they hold any other place or office, or receive any pension or salary from any other State, or government, or power, whatever.

No person shall be capable of holding or exercising at the same time, within this State, more than one of the following offices, viz: judge of probate, sheriff, register of probate, or register of deeds; and never more than any two offices, which are to be held by appointment of the governor, or the governor and council, or the senate, or the house of representatives, or by the election of the people of the State at large, or of the people of any county, military offices, and the offices of justices of the peace excepted, shall be held by one person.

No person holding the office of judge of the supreme judicial court, secretary, attorney-general, solicitor-general, treasurer or receiver-general, judge of probate, commissary-general, president, professor, or instructor of Harvard College, sheriff, clerk of the house of representatives, register of probate, register of deeds, clerk of the supreme judicial court, clerk of the inferior court of common pleas, or officer of the customs, including in this description naval officers, shall at the same time have a seat in the senate or house of representatives; but their being chosen or appointed to, and accepting the same, shall operate as a resignation of their seat in the senate or house of representatives; and the place so vacated shall be filled up.

And the same rule shall take place in case any judge of the said supreme judicial court or judge of probate shall accept a seat in council, or any councillor shall accept of either of those offices or places.

And no person shall ever be admitted to hold a seat in the legislature, or any office of trust or importance under the government of this commonwealth, who shall in the due course of law have been convicted of bribery or corruption in obtaining an election or appointment.

Art. III. In all cases where sums or money are mentioned in this constitution, the value thereof shall be computed in silver, at six shillings and eight pence per ounce; and it shall in the power of the legislature, from time to time, to increase such qualifications, as to property, of the persons to be elected to offices as the circumstances of the commonwealth shall require.

Art. IV. All commissions shall be in the name of the commonwealth of Massachusetts, signed by the governor, and attested by the secretary or his deputy, and have the great seal of the commonwealth affixed thereto.

Art. V. All writs, issuing of the clerk's office in any of the courts of law, shall be in the name of the commonwealth of Massachusetts; they shall be under the seal of the court from when they issue; they shall bear test of the first justice of the court to which they shall be returned who is not a party, and be signed by the clerk of such court.

Art. VI. All the laws which have heretofore been adopted, used, and approved in the province, colony, or State of Massachusetts Bay, and usually practiced on in the courts of law, shall still remain and be in full force, until altered or repealed by the legislature, such parts only excepted as are repugnant to the rights and liberties contained in this constitution.

Art. VII. The privilege and benefit of the writ of *habeas corpus* shall be enjoyed in this commonwealth, in the most free, easy, cheap, expeditious, and ample manner, and shall not be suspended by the legislature, except upon the most urgent and pressing occasions, and for a limited time, not exceeding twelve months.

Art. VIII. The enacting style, in making and passing all acts, statutes, and laws, shall be, *"Be it enacted by the senate and house of representatives in general court assembled, and by authority of the same."*

Art. IX. To the end there may be no failure of justice or danger arise to the commonwealth from a change in the form of government, all officers, civil and military, holding commissions under the government and people of Massachusetts Bay, in New England, and all other officers of the said government and people, at the time this constitution shall take effect, shall have, hold, use, exercise, and enjoy all the powers and authority to them granted or committed until other persons shall be appointed in their stead; and all courts of law shall proceed in the execution of the business of their respective departments; and all the executive and legislative officers, bodies, and powers shall continue in full force, in the enjoyment and exercise of all their trusts, employments, and authority, until the general court, and the supreme and executive officers under this constitution, are designated and invested with their respective trusts, powers, and authority.

Art. X. In order the more effectually to adhere to the principles of the constitution, and to correct those violations which by any means may be made therein, as well as to form such alterations as from experience shall be found necessary, the general court which shall be in the year of our Lord [1795] shall issue precepts to the selectmen of the several towns, and to the assessors of the unincorporated plantations, directing them to convene the qualified voters of their respective towns and plantations, for the purpose of collecting their sentiments on the necessity or expediency of revising the constitution in order to amendments.

And if it shall appear, by the returns made, that two-thirds of the qualified voters throughout the State, who shall assemble and vote in consequence of the said precepts, are in favor of such revision or amendment, the general court shall issue precepts, or direct them to be issued from the secretary's office, to the several towns to elect or direct them to be issued from the secretary's office, to the several towns to elect delegates to meet in convention for the purpose aforesaid.

And said delegates to be chosen in the same manner and proportion as their representatives in the second branch of the legislature are by this constitution to be chosen.

Art. XI. This form of government shall be enrolled on parchment and deposited in the secretary's office, and be a part of the laws of the land, and printed copies thereof shall be prefixed to the book containing the laws of this commonwealth in all future editions of the said laws.

JAMES BOWDOIN, *President*
Samuel Barrett, *Secretary*

LESSON EIGHT

THE ARTICLES OF CONFEDERATION

Articles of Confederation

(March 1, 1781)

Congress of the Confederation

▌The History[8*]

Before the Constitution there was the Articles of Confederation –– in effect, the first constitution of the United States. Drafted in 1777 by the same Continental Congress that passed the Declaration of Independence, the articles established a "firm league of friendship" between and among the 13 states.

Created during the throes of the Revolutionary War, the Articles reflect the wariness by the states of a strong central government. Afraid that their individual needs would be ignored by a national government with too much power, and the abuses that often result from such power, the Articles purposely established a "constitution" that vested the largest share of power to the individual states.

Under the Articles each of the states retained their "sovereignty, freedom, and independence." Instead of setting up executive and judicial branches of government, there was a committee of delegates composed of representatives from each state. These individuals comprised the Congress, a national legislature called for by the Articles.

The Congress was responsible for conducting foreign affairs, declaring war or peace, maintaining an army and navy and a variety of other lesser functions. But the Articles denied Congress the power to collect taxes, regulate interstate commerce and enforce laws.

Eventually, these shortcomings would lead to the adoption of the U.S. Constitution. But during those years in which the 13 states were struggling to achieve their independent status, the Articles of Confederation stood them in good stead.

Adopted by Congress on November 15, 1777, the Articles became operative on March 1, 1781 when the last of the 13 states signed on to the document.

---

[8] * Originally published as "The Articles of Confederation and Perpetual Union," *Early America's Milestone Historic Documents*, Archiving Early America, Seattle, Washington, 2009. For additional information see "The First Constitution –– The Articles of Confederation," *The Charters of Freedom*, U.S. National Archives and Records Administration, College Park, Maryland, 2004. This agency is listed in the *National Resource Directory* section of this volume.

▌The Document

Articles of Confederation

To all to whom these Presents shall come, we the undersigned Delegates of the States affixed to our Names send greeting.

Articles of Confederation and perpetual Union between the states of New Hampshire, Massachusetts-bay Rhode Island and Providence Plantations, Connecticut, New York, New Jersey, Pennsylvania, Delaware, Maryland, Virginia, North Carolina, South Carolina and Georgia.

I. The Stile of this Confederacy shall be "The United States of America."

II. Each state retains its sovereignty, freedom, and independence, and every power, jurisdiction, and right, which is not by this Confederation expressly delegated to the United States, in Congress assembled.

III. The said States hereby severally enter into a firm league of friendship with each other, for their common defense, the security of their liberties, and their mutual and general welfare, binding themselves to assist each other, against all force offered to, or attacks made upon them, or any of them, on account of religion, sovereignty, trade, or any other pretense whatever.

IV. The better to secure and perpetuate mutual friendship and intercourse among the people of the different States in this Union, the free inhabitants of each of these States, paupers, vagabonds, and fugitives from justice excepted, shall be entitled to all privileges and immunities of free citizens in the several States; and the people of each State shall free ingress and regress to and from any other State, and shall enjoy therein all the privileges of trade and commerce, subject to the same duties, impositions, and restrictions as the inhabitants thereof respectively, provided that such restrictions shall not extend so far as to prevent the removal of property imported into any State, to any other State, of which the owner is an inhabitant; provided also that no imposition, duties or restriction shall be laid by any State, on the property of the United States, or either of them.

If any person guilty of, or charged with, treason, felony, or other high misdemeanor in any State, shall flee from justice, and be found in any of the United States, he shall, upon demand of the Governor or executive power of the State from which he fled, be delivered up and removed to the State having jurisdiction of his offense.

Full faith and credit shall be given in each of these States to the records, acts, and judicial proceedings of the courts and magistrates of every other State.

V. For the most convenient management of the general interests of the United States, delegates shall be annually appointed in such manner as the legislatures of each State shall direct, to meet in Congress on the first Monday in November, in every year, with a power reserved to each State to recall its delegates, or any of them, at any time within the year, and to send others in their stead for the remainder of the year.

No State shall be represented in Congress by less than two, nor more than seven members; and no person shall be capable of being a delegate for more than three years in any term of six years; nor shall any person, being a delegate, be capable of holding any office under the United States, for which he, or another for his benefit, receives any salary, fees or emolument of any kind.

Each State shall maintain its own delegates in a meeting of the States, and while they act as members of the committee of the States.

In determining questions in the United States in Congress assembled, each State shall have one vote.

Freedom of speech and debate in Congress shall not be impeached or questioned in any court or place out of Congress, and the members of Congress shall be protected in their persons from arrests or imprisonments, during the time of their going to and from, and attendence on Congress, except for treason, felony, or breach of the peace.

VI. No State, without the consent of the United States in Congress assembled, shall send any embassy to, or receive any embassy from, or enter into any conference, agreement, alliance or treaty with any King, Prince or State; nor shall any person holding any office of profit or trust under the United States, or any of them, accept any present, emolument, office or title of any kind whatever from any King, Prince or foreign State; nor shall the United States in Congress assembled, or any of them, grant any title of nobility.

No two or more States shall enter into any treaty, confederation or alliance whatever between them, without the consent of the United States in Congress assembled, specifying accurately the purposes for which the same is to be entered into, and how long it shall continue.

No State shall lay any imposts or duties, which may interfere with any stipulations in treaties, entered into by the United States in Congress assembled, with any King, Prince or State, in pursuance of any treaties already proposed by Congress, to the courts of France and Spain.

No vessel of war shall be kept up in time of peace by any State, except such number only, as shall be deemed necessary by the United States in Congress assembled, for the defense of such State, or its trade; nor shall any body of forces be kept up by any State in time of peace, except such number only, as in the judgement of the United States in Congress assembled, shall be deemed requisite to garrison the forts necessary for the defense of such State; but every State shall always keep up a well-regulated and disciplined militia, sufficiently armed and accoutered, and shall provide and constantly have ready for use, in public stores, a due number of filed pieces and tents, and a proper quantity of arms, ammunition and camp equipage.

No State shall engage in any war without the consent of the United States in Congress assembled, unless such State be actually invaded by enemies, or shall have received certain advice of a resolution being formed by some nation of Indians to invade such State, and the danger is so imminent as not to admit of a delay till the United States in Congress assembled can be consulted; nor shall any State grant commissions to any ships or vessels of war, nor letters of marque or reprisal, except it be after a declaration of war by the United States in Congress assembled, and then only against the Kingdom or State and the subjects thereof, against which war has been so declared, and under such regulations as shall be established by the United States in Congress assembled, unless such State be infested by pirates, in which case vessels of war may be fitted out for that occasion, and kept so long as the danger shall continue, or until the United States in Congress assembled shall determine otherwise.

VII. When land forces are raised by any State for the common defense, all officers of or under the rank of colonel, shall be appointed by the legislature of each State respectively, by whom such forces shall be raised, or in such manner as such State shall direct, and all vacancies shall be filled up by the State which first made the appointment.

VIII. All charges of war, and all other expenses that shall be incurred for the common defense or general welfare, and allowed by the United States in Congress assembled, shall be defrayed out of a common treasury, which shall be supplied by the several States in proportion to the value of all land within each State, granted or surveyed for any person, as such land and the buildings and improvements thereon shall be estimated according to such mode as the United States in Congress assembled, shall from time to time direct and appoint.

The taxes for paying that proportion shall be laid and levied by the authority and direction of the legislatures of the several States within the time agreed upon by the United States in Congress assembled.

IX. The United States in Congress assembled, shall have the sole and exclusive right and power of determining on peace and war, except in the cases mentioned in the sixth article –– of sending and receiving ambassadors –– entering into treaties and alliances, provided that no treaty of commerce shall be made whereby the legislative power of the respective States shall be restrained from imposing such imposts and duties on foreigners, as their own people are subjected to, or from prohibiting the exportation or importation of any species of goods or commodities whatsoever –– of establishing rules for deciding in all cases, what captures on land or water shall be legal, and in what manner prizes taken by land or naval forces in the service of the United States shall be divided or appropriated –– of granting letters of marque and reprisal in times of peace –– appointing courts for the trial of piracies and felonies committed on the high seas and establishing courts for receiving and determining finally appeals in all cases of captures, provided that no member of Congress shall be appointed a judge of any of the said courts.

The United States in Congress assembled shall also be the last resort on appeal in all disputes and differences now subsisting or that hereafter may arise between two or more States concerning boundary, jurisdiction or any other causes whatever; which authority shall always be exercised in the manner following. Whenever the legislative or executive authority or lawful agent of any State in controversy with another shall present a petition to Congress stating the matter in question and praying for a hearing, notice thereof shall be given by order of Congress to the legislative or executive authority of the other State in controversy, and a day assigned for the appearance of the parties by their lawful agents, who shall then be directed to appoint by joint consent, commissioners or judges to constitute a court for hearing and determining the matter in question: but if they cannot agree, Congress shall name three persons out of each of the United States, and from the list of such persons each party shall alternately strike out one, the petitioners beginning, until the number shall be reduced to thirteen; and from that number not less than seven, nor more than nine names as Congress shall direct, shall in the presence of Congress be drawn out by lot, and the persons whose names shall be so drawn or any five of them, shall be commissioners or judges, to hear and finally determine the controversy, so always as a major part of the judges who shall hear the cause shall agree in the determination: and if either party shall neglect to attend at the day appointed, without showing reasons, which Congress shall judge sufficient, or being present shall refuse to strike, the Congress shall proceed to nominate three persons out of each State, and the secretary of Congress shall strike in behalf of such party absent or refusing; and the judgement and sentence of the court to be appointed, in the manner before prescribed, shall be final and conclusive; and if any of the parties shall refuse to submit to the authority of such court, or to appear or defend their claim or cause, the court shall nevertheless proceed to pronounce sentence, or judgement, which shall in like manner be final and decisive, the judgement or sentence and other proceedings being in either case transmitted to Congress, and lodged among the acts of Congress for the security of the parties concerned: provided that every commissioner, before he sits in judgement, shall take an oath to be administered by one of the judges of the supreme or superior court of the State, where the cause shall be tried, 'well and truly to hear and determine the matter in question, according to the best of his judgement, without favor, affection or hope of reward': provided also, that no State shall be deprived of territory for the benefit of the United States.

All controversies concerning the private right of soil claimed under different grants of two or more States, whose jurisdictions as they may respect such lands, and the States which passed such grants are adjusted, the said grants or either of them being at the same time claimed to have originated antecedent to such settlement of jurisdiction, shall on the petition of either party to the Congress of the United States, be finally determined as near as may be in the same manner as is before presecribed for deciding disputes respecting territorial jurisdiction between different States.

The United States in Congress assembled shall also have the sole and exclusive right and power of regulating the alloy and value of coin struck by their own authority, or by that of the respective States — fixing the standards of weights and measures throughout the United States — regulating the trade and managing all affairs with the Indians, not members of any of the States, provided that the legislative right of any State within its own limits be not infringed or violated — establishing or regulating post offices from one State to another, throughout all the United States, and exacting such postage on the papers passing through the same as may be requisite to defray the expenses of the said office — appointing all officers of the land forces, in the service of the United States, excepting regimental officers — appointing all the officers of the naval forces, and commissioning all officers whatever in the service of the United States — making rules for the government and regulation of the said land and naval forces, and directing their operations.

The United States in Congress assembled shall have authority to appoint a committee, to sit in the recess of Congress, to be denominated 'A Committee of the States,' and to consist of one delegate from each State; and to appoint such other committees and civil officers as may be necessary for managing the general affairs of the United States under their direction — to appoint one of their members to preside, provided that no person be allowed to serve in the office of president more than one year in any term of three years; to ascertain the necessary sums of money to be raised for the service of the United States, and to appropriate and apply the same for defraying the public expenses — to borrow money, or emit bills on the credit of the United States, transmitting every half-year to the respective States an account of the sums of money so borrowed or emitted — to build and equip a navy — to agree upon the number of land forces, and to make requisitions from each State for its quota, in proportion to the number of white inhabitants in such State; which requisition shall be binding, and thereupon the legislature of each State shall appoint the regimental officers, raise the men and cloath, arm and equip them in a solid-like manner, at the expense of the United States; and the officers and men so cloathed, armed and equipped shall march to the place appointed, and within the time agreed on by the United States in Congress assembled. But if the United States in Congress assembled shall, on consideration of circumstances judge proper that any State should not raise men, or should raise a smaller number of men than the quota thereof, such extra number shall be raised, officered, cloathed, armed and equipped in the same manner as the quota of each State, unless the legislature of such State shall judge that such extra number cannot be safely spread out in the same, in which case they shall raise, officer, cloath, arm and equip as many of such extra number as they judge can be safely spared. And the officers and men so cloathed, armed, and equipped, shall march to the place appointed, and within the time agreed on by the United States in Congress assembled.

The United States in Congress assembled shall never engage in a war, nor grant letters of marque or reprisal in time of peace, nor enter into any treaties or alliances, nor coin money, nor regulate the value thereof, nor ascertain the sums and expenses necessary for the defense and welfare of the United States, or any of them, nor emit bills, nor borrow money on the credit of the United States, nor appropriate money, nor agree upon the number of vessels of war, to be built or purchased, or the number of land or sea forces to be raised, nor appoint a commander in chief of the army or navy, unless nine States assent to the same: nor shall a question on any other point, except for adjourning from day to day be determined, unless by the votes of the majority of the United States in Congress assembled.

The Congress of the United States shall have power to adjourn to any time within the year, and to any place within the United States, so that no period of adjournment be for a longer duration than the space of six months, and shall publish the journal of their proceedings monthly, except such parts thereof relating to treaties, alliances or military operations, as in their judgement require secrecy; and the yeas and nays of the delegates of each State on any question shall be entered on the journal, when it is desired by any delegates of a State, or any of them, at his or their request shall be furnished with a transcript of the said journal, except such parts as are above excepted, to lay before the legislatures of the several States.

X. The Committee of the States, or any nine of them, shall be authorized to execute, in the recess of Congress, such of the powers of Congress as the United States in Congress assembled, by the consent of the nine States, shall from time to time think expedient to vest them with; provided that no power be delegated to the said Committee, for the exercise of which, by the Articles of Confederation, the voice of nine States in the Congress of the United States assembled be requisite.

XI. Canada acceding to this confederation, and adjoining in the measures of the United States, shall be admitted into, and entitled to all the advantages of this Union; but no other colony shall be admitted into the same, unless such admission be agreed to by nine States.

XII. All bills of credit emitted, monies borrowed, and debts contracted by, or under the authority of Congress, before the assembling of the United States, in pursuance of the present confederation, shall be deemed and considered as a charge against the United States, for payment and satisfaction whereof the said United States, and the public faith are hereby solemnly pleged.

XIII. Every State shall abide by the determination of the United States in Congress assembled, on all questions which by this confederation are submitted to them. And the Articles of this Confederation shall be inviolably observed by every State, and the Union shall be perpetual; nor shall any alteration at any time hereafter be made in any of them; unless such alteration be agreed to in a Congress of the United States, and be afterwards confirmed by the legislatures of every State.

And whereas it hath pleased the Great Governor of the World to incline the hearts of the legislatures we respectively represent in Congress, to approve of, and to authorize us to ratify the said Articles of Confederation and perpetual Union. Know Ye that we the undersigned delegates, by virtue of the power and authority to us given for that purpose, do by these presents, in the name and in behalf of our respective constituents, fully and entirely ratify and confirm each and every of the said Articles of Confederation and perpetual Union, and all and singular the matters and things therein contained: And we do further solemnly plight and engage the faith of our respective constituents, that they shall abide by the determinations of the United States in Congress assembled, on all questions, which by the said Confederation are submitted to them. And that the Articles thereof shall be inviolably observed by the States we respectively represent, and that the Union shall be perpetual.

In Witness whereof we have hereunto set our hands in Congress. Done at Philadelphia in the State of Pennsylvania the ninth day of July in the Year of our Lord One Thousand Seven Hundred and Seventy-Eight, and in the Third Year of the independence of America.

Agreed to by Congress 15 November 1777. In force after ratification by Maryland, 1 March 1781.

LESSON NINE

THE CONSTITUTION OF THE UNITED STATES

Constitution of the United States

(September 17, 1787)

Congress of the Confederation

▌The History[9]*

The Constitution of the United States of America is the supreme law of the United States. It is the foundation and source of the legal authority underlying the existence of the United States of America and the Federal Government of the United States. It provides the framework for the organization of the United States Government. The document defines the three main branches of the government: The legislative branch with a bicameral Congress, an executive branch led by the President, and a judicial branch headed by the Supreme Court. Besides providing for the organization of these branches, the Constitution outlines obligations of each office, as well as provides what powers each branch may exercise. It also reserves numerous rights for the individual states, thereby establishing the United States' federal system of government. It is the shortest and oldest written constitution of any major sovereign state.

The United States Constitution was adopted on September 17, 1787, by the Constitutional Convention (or Constitutional Congress) in Philadelphia, Pennsylvania, and later ratified by conventions in each U.S. state in the name of "The People"; it has since been amended twenty-seven times, the first ten amendments being known as the Bill of Rights. The Articles of Confederation and Perpetual Union was actually the first constitution of the United States of America. The U.S. Constitution replaced the Articles of Confederation as the governing document for the United States after being ratified by nine states. The Constitution has a central place in United States law and political culture. The handwritten, or "engrossed," original document penned by Jacob Shallus is on display at the National Archives and Records Administration in Washington, D.C.

In September 1786, commissioners from five states met in the Annapolis Convention to discuss adjustments to the Articles of Confederation that would improve commerce. They invited state representatives to convene in Philadelphia to discuss improvements to the federal government. After debate, the Congress of the Confederation endorsed the plan to revise the Articles of Confederation on February 21, 1787. Twelve states, Rhode Island being the only exception, accepted this invitation and sent delegates to convene in May 1787. The resolution calling the Convention specified that its purpose was to propose amendments to the Articles, but through discussion and debate it became clear by mid–June that, rather than amend the existing Articles, the Convention decided to propose a rewritten Constitution.

---

[9] * Originally published as "United States Constitution," *Wikipedia*, Wikimedia Foundation, Inc., San Francisco, California, November 2009. For additional information see "Constitution of the United States," *The Charters of Freedom*, U.S. National Archives and Records Administration, College Park, Maryland, 2004. This agency is listed in the *National Resource Directory* section of this volume.

The Philadelphia Convention voted to keep the debates secret, so that the delegates could speak freely. They also decided to draft a new fundamental government design. Despite Article 13 of the Articles of Confederation stating that the union created under the Articles was "perpetual" and that any alteration must be "agreed to in a Congress of the United States, and be afterwards confirmed by the legislatures of every State," Article VII of the proposed constitution stipulated that only nine of the thirteen states would have to ratify for the new government to go into effect (for the participating states). Current knowledge of the drafting and construction of the United States Constitution comes primarily from the diaries left by James Madison, who kept a complete record of the proceedings at the Constitutional Convention.

The Virginia Plan was the unofficial agenda for the Convention, and was drafted chiefly by James Madison, considered to be "The Father of the Constitution" for his major contributions. It was weighted toward the interests of the larger states, and proposed among other points:

- A powerful bicameral legislature with a House and a Senate
- An executive chosen by the legislature
- A judiciary, with life-terms of service and vague powers
- The national legislature would be able to veto state laws

An alternate proposal, William Paterson's New Jersey Plan, gave states equal weights and was supported by the smaller states. Roger Sherman of Connecticut brokered The Great Compromise whereby the House would represent the people, a Senate would represent the states, and a president would be elected by electors.

The contentious issue of slavery was too controversial to be resolved during the convention. As a result, the original Constitution contained four provisions tacitly allowing slavery to continue for the next 20 years. Section 9 of Article I allowed the continued "importation" of such persons, Section 2 of Article IV prohibited the provision of assistance to escaping persons and required their return if successful and Section 2 of Article I defined other persons as "three-fifths" of a person for calculations of each state's official population for representation for federal taxation. Article V prohibited any amendments or legislation changing the provision regarding slave importation until 1808, thereby giving the States then existing 20 years to resolve this issue. The failure to do so was a contributing factor to the Civil War.

Contrary to the process for "alteration" spelled out in Article 13 of the Articles, Congress submitted the proposal to the states and set the terms for representation.

On September 17, 1787, the Constitution was completed in Philadelphia at the Federal Convention, followed by a speech given by Benjamin Franklin who urged unanimity, although they decided only nine states were needed to ratify the constitution for it to go into effect. The Convention submitted the Constitution to the Congress of the Confederation, where it received approval according to Article 13 of the Articles of Confederation.

Once the Congress of the Confederation received word of New Hampshire's ratification, it set a timetable for the start of operations under the Constitution, and on March 4, 1789, the government under the Constitution began operations.

The Document[10]*

Constitution of the United States

We the People of the United States, in Order to form a more perfect Union, establish Justice, insure domestic Tranquility, provide for the common defense, promote the general Welfare, and secure the Blessings of Liberty to ourselves and our Posterity, do ordain and establish this Constitution for the United States of America.

ARTICLE. I

Section. 1.

All legislative Powers herein granted shall be vested in a Congress of the United States, which shall consist of a Senate and House of Representatives.

Section. 2.

The House of Representatives shall be composed of Members chosen every second Year by the People of the several States, and the Electors in each State shall have the Qualifications requisite for Electors of the most numerous Branch of the State Legislature.

No Person shall be a Representative who shall not have attained to the Age of twenty five Years, and been seven Years a Citizen of the United States, and who shall not, when elected, be an Inhabitant of that State in which he shall be chosen.

Representatives and direct Taxes shall be apportioned among the several States which may be included within this Union, according to their respective Numbers, which shall be determined by adding to the whole Number of free Persons, including those bound to Service for a Term of Years, and excluding Indians not taxed, three fifths of all other Persons. The actual Enumeration shall be made within three Years after the first Meeting of the Congress of the United States, and within every subsequent Term of ten Years, in such Manner as they shall by Law direct. The Number of Representatives shall not exceed one for every thirty Thousand, but each State shall have at Least one Representative; and until such enumeration shall be made, the State of New Hampshire shall be entitled to chuse three, Massachusetts eight, Rhode-Island and Providence Plantations one, Connecticut five, New-York six, New Jersey four, Pennsylvania eight, Delaware one, Maryland six, Virginia ten, North Carolina five, South Carolina five, and Georgia three.

When vacancies happen in the Representation from any State, the Executive Authority thereof shall issue Writs of Election to fill such Vacancies.

The House of Representatives shall chuse their Speaker and other Officers; and shall have the sole Power of Impeachment.

---

[10] * The text following is a transcription of the U.S. Constitution in its original form. Items that are underlined have since been either amended or superseded.

Section. 3.

The Senate of the United States shall be composed of two Senators from each State, <u>chosen by the Legislature</u> thereof for six Years; and each Senator shall have one Vote.

Immediately after they shall be assembled in Consequence of the first Election, they shall be divided as equally as may be into three Classes. The Seats of the Senators of the first Class shall be vacated at the Expiration of the second Year, of the second Class at the Expiration of the fourth Year, and of the third Class at the Expiration of the sixth Year, so that one third may be chosen every second Year; <u>and if Vacancies happen by Resignation, or otherwise, during the Recess of the Legislature of any State, the Executive thereof may make temporary Appointments until the next Meeting of the Legislature, which shall then fill such Vacancies.</u>

No Person shall be a Senator who shall not have attained to the Age of thirty Years, and been nine Years a Citizen of the United States, and who shall not, when elected, be an Inhabitant of that State for which he shall be chosen.

The Vice President of the United States shall be President of the Senate, but shall have no Vote, unless they be equally divided.

The Senate shall chuse their other Officers, and also a President pro tempore, in the Absence of the Vice President, or when he shall exercise the Office of President of the United States.

The Senate shall have the sole Power to try all Impeachments. When sitting for that Purpose, they shall be on Oath or Affirmation. When the President of the United States is tried, the Chief Justice shall preside: And no Person shall be convicted without the Concurrence of two thirds of the Members present.

Judgment in Cases of Impeachment shall not extend further than to removal from Office, and disqualification to hold and enjoy any Office of honor, Trust or Profit under the United States: but the Party convicted shall nevertheless be liable and subject to Indictment, Trial, Judgment and Punishment, according to Law.

Section. 4.

The Times, Places and Manner of holding Elections for Senators and Representatives, shall be prescribed in each State by the Legislature thereof; but the Congress may at any time by Law make or alter such Regulations, except as to the Places of chusing Senators.

The Congress shall assemble at least once in every Year, and such Meeting shall <u>be on the first Monday in December,</u> unless they shall by Law appoint a different Day.

Section. 5.

Each House shall be the Judge of the Elections, Returns and Qualifications of its own Members, and a Majority of each shall constitute a Quorum to do Business; but a smaller Number may adjourn from day to day, and may be authorized to compel the Attendance of absent Members, in such Manner, and under such Penalties as each House may provide.

Each House may determine the Rules of its Proceedings, punish its Members for disorderly Behaviour, and, with the Concurrence of two thirds, expel a Member.

Each House shall keep a Journal of its Proceedings, and from time to time publish the same, excepting such Parts as may in their Judgment require Secrecy; and the Yeas and Nays of the Members of either House on any question shall, at the Desire of one fifth of those Present, be entered on the Journal.

Neither House, during the Session of Congress, shall, without the Consent of the other, adjourn for more than three days, nor to any other Place than that in which the two Houses shall be sitting.

Section. 6.

The Senators and Representatives shall receive a Compensation for their Services, to be ascertained by Law, and paid out of the Treasury of the United States. They shall in all Cases, except Treason, Felony and Breach of the Peace, be privileged from Arrest during their Attendance at the Session of their respective Houses, and in going to and returning from the same; and for any Speech or Debate in either House, they shall not be questioned in any other Place.

No Senator or Representative shall, during the Time for which he was elected, be appointed to any civil Office under the Authority of the United States, which shall have been created, or the Emoluments whereof shall have been encreased during such time; and no Person holding any Office under the United States, shall be a Member of either House during his Continuance in Office.

Section. 7.

All Bills for raising Revenue shall originate in the House of Representatives; but the Senate may propose or concur with Amendments as on other Bills.

Every Bill which shall have passed the House of Representatives and the Senate, shall, before it become a Law, be presented to the President of the United States: If he approves he shall sign it, but if not he shall return it, with his Objections to that House in which it shall have originated, who shall enter the Objections at large on their Journal, and proceed to reconsider it. If after such Reconsideration two thirds of that House shall agree to pass the Bill, it shall be sent, together with the Objections, to the other House, by which it shall likewise be reconsidered, and if approved by two thirds of that House, it shall become a Law. But in all such Cases the Votes of both Houses shall be determined by yeas and Nays, and the Names of the Persons voting for and against the Bill shall be entered on the Journal of each House respectively. If any Bill shall not be returned by the President within ten Days (Sundays excepted) after it shall have been presented to him, the Same shall be a Law, in like Manner as if he had signed it, unless the Congress by their Adjournment prevent its Return, in which Case it shall not be a Law.

Every Order, Resolution, or Vote to which the Concurrence of the Senate and House of Representatives may be necessary (except on a question of Adjournment) shall be presented to the President of the United States; and before the Same shall take Effect, shall be approved by him, or being disapproved by him, shall be repassed by two thirds of the Senate and House of Representatives, according to the Rules and Limitations prescribed in the Case of a Bill.

Section. 8.

The Congress shall have Power To lay and collect Taxes, Duties, Imposts and Excises, to pay the Debts and provide for the common Defence and general Welfare of the United States; but all Duties, Imposts and Excises shall be uniform throughout the United States;

To borrow Money on the credit of the United States;

To regulate Commerce with foreign Nations, and among the several States, and with the Indian Tribes;

To establish an uniform Rule of Naturalization, and uniform Laws on the subject of Bankruptcies throughout the United States;

To coin Money, regulate the Value thereof, and of foreign Coin, and fix the Standard of Weights and Measures;

To provide for the Punishment of counterfeiting the Securities and current Coin of the United States;

To establish Post Offices and post Roads;

To promote the Progress of Science and useful Arts, by securing for limited Times to Authors and Inventors the exclusive Right to their respective Writings and Discoveries;

To constitute Tribunals inferior to the supreme Court;

To define and punish Piracies and Felonies committed on the high Seas, and Offences against the Law of Nations;

To declare War, grant Letters of Marque and Reprisal, and make Rules concerning Captures on Land and Water;

To raise and support Armies, but no Appropriation of Money to that Use shall be for a longer Term than two Years;

To provide and maintain a Navy;

To make Rules for the Government and Regulation of the land and naval Forces;

To provide for calling forth the Militia to execute the Laws of the Union, suppress Insurrections and repel Invasions;

To provide for organizing, arming, and disciplining, the Militia, and for governing such Part of them as may be employed in the Service of the United States, reserving to the States respectively, the Appointment of the Officers, and the Authority of training the Militia according to the discipline prescribed by Congress;

To exercise exclusive Legislation in all Cases whatsoever, over such District (not exceeding ten Miles square) as may, by Cession of particular States, and the Acceptance of Congress, become the Seat of the Government of the United States, and to exercise like Authority over all Places purchased by the Consent of the Legislature of the State in which the Same shall be, for the Erection of Forts, Magazines, Arsenals, dock-Yards, and other needful Buildings; –– And

To make all Laws which shall be necessary and proper for carrying into Execution the foregoing Powers, and all other Powers vested by this Constitution in the Government of the United States, or in any Department or Officer thereof.

Section. 9.

The Migration or Importation of such Persons as any of the States now existing shall think proper to admit, shall not be prohibited by the Congress prior to the Year one thousand eight hundred and eight, but a Tax or duty may be imposed on such Importation, not exceeding ten dollars for each Person.

The Privilege of the Writ of Habeas Corpus shall not be suspended, unless when in Cases of Rebellion or Invasion the public Safety may require it.

No Bill of Attainder or ex post facto Law shall be passed.

No Capitation, or other direct, Tax shall be laid, <u>unless in Proportion to the Census or enumeration herein before directed to be taken.</u>

No Tax or Duty shall be laid on Articles exported from any State.

No Preference shall be given by any Regulation of Commerce or Revenue to the Ports of one State over those of another; nor shall Vessels bound to, or from, one State, be obliged to enter, clear, or pay Duties in a other.

No Money shall be drawn from the Treasury, but in Consequence of Appropriations made by Law; and a regular Statement and Account of the Receipts and Expenditures of all public Money shall be published from time to time.

No Title of Nobility shall be granted by the United States: And no Person holding any Office of Profit or Trust under them, shall, without the Consent of the Congress, accept of any present, Emolument, Office, or Title, of any kind whatever, from any King, Prince, or foreign State.

Section. 10.

No State shall enter into any Treaty, Alliance, or Confederation; grant Letters of Marque and Reprisal; coin Money; emit Bills of Credit; make any Thing but gold and silver Coin a Tender in Payment of Debts; pass any Bill of Attainder, ex post facto Law, or Law impairing the Obligation of Contracts, or grant any Title of Nobility.

No State shall, without the Consent of the Congress, lay any Imposts or Duties on Imports or Exports, except what may be absolutely necessary for executing it's inspection Laws: and the net Produce of all Duties and Imposts, laid by any State on Imports or Exports, shall be for the Use of the Treasury of the United States; and all such Laws shall be subject to the Revision and Controul of the Congress.

No State shall, without the Consent of Congress, lay any Duty of Tonnage, keep Troops, or Ships of War in time of Peace, enter into any Agreement or Compact with another State, or with a foreign Power, or engage in War, unless actually invaded, or in such imminent Danger as will not admit of delay.

ARTICLE. II.

Section. 1.

The executive Power shall be vested in a President of the United States of America. He shall hold his Office during the Term of four Years, and, together with the Vice President, chosen for the same Term, be elected, as follows:

Each State shall appoint, in such Manner as the Legislature thereof may direct, a Number of Electors, equal to the whole Number of Senators and Representatives to which the State may be entitled in the Congress: but no Senator or Representative, or Person holding an Office of Trust or Profit under the United States, shall be appointed an Elector.

The Electors shall meet in their respective States, and vote by Ballot for two Persons, of whom one at least shall not be an Inhabitant of the same State with themselves. And they shall make a List of all the Persons voted for, and of the Number of Votes for each; which List they shall sign and certify, and transmit sealed to the Seat of the Government of the United States, directed to the President of the Senate. The President of the Senate shall, in the Presence of the Senate and House of Representatives, open all the Certificates, and the Votes shall then be counted. The Person having the greatest Number of Votes shall be the President, if such Number be a Majority of the whole Number of Electors appointed; and if there be more than one who have such Majority, and have an equal Number of Votes, then the House of Representatives shall immediately chuse by Ballot one of them for President; and if no Person have a Majority, then from the five highest on the List the said House shall in like Manner chuse the President. But in chusing the President, the Votes shall be taken by States, the Representation from each State having one Vote; A quorum for this purpose shall consist of a Member or Members from two thirds of the States, and a Majority of all the States shall be necessary to a Choice. In every Case, after the Choice of the President, the Person having the greatest Number of Votes of the Electors shall be the Vice President. But if there should remain two or more who have equal Votes, the Senate shall chuse from them by Ballot the Vice President.

The Congress may determine the Time of chusing the Electors, and the Day on which they shall give their Votes; which Day shall be the same throughout the United States.

No Person except a natural born Citizen, or a Citizen of the United States, at the time of the Adoption of this Constitution, shall be eligible to the Office of President; neither shall any Person be eligible to that Office who shall not have attained to the Age of thirty five Years, and been fourteen Years a Resident within the United States.

In Case of the Removal of the President from Office, or of his Death, Resignation, or Inability to discharge the Powers and Duties of the said Office, the Same shall devolve on the Vice President, and the Congress may by Law provide for the Case of Removal, Death, Resignation or Inability, both of the President and Vice President, declaring what Officer shall then act as President, and such Officer shall act accordingly, until the Disability be removed, or a President shall be elected.

The President shall, at stated Times, receive for his Services, a Compensation, which shall neither be increased nor diminished during the Period for which he shall have been elected, and he shall not receive within that Period any other Emolument from the United States, or any of them.

Before he enter on the Execution of his Office, he shall take the following Oath or Affirmation: –– "I do solemnly swear (or affirm) that I will faithfully execute the Office of President of the United States, and will to the best of my Ability, preserve, protect and defend the Constitution of the United States."

Section. 2.

The President shall be Commander in Chief of the Army and Navy of the United States, and of the Militia of the several States, when called into the actual Service of the United States; he may require the Opinion, in writing, of the principal Officer in each of the executive Departments, upon any Subject relating to the Duties of their respective Offices, and he shall have Power to grant Reprieves and Pardons for Offences against the United States, except in Cases of Impeachment.

He shall have Power, by and with the Advice and Consent of the Senate, to make Treaties, provided two thirds of the Senators present concur; and he shall nominate, and by and with the Advice and Consent of the Senate, shall appoint Ambassadors, other public Ministers and Consuls, Judges of the supreme Court, and all other Officers of the United States, whose Appointments are not herein otherwise provided for, and which shall be established by Law: but the Congress may by Law vest the Appointment of such inferior Officers, as they think proper, in the President alone, in the Courts of Law, or in the Heads of Departments.

The President shall have Power to fill up all Vacancies that may happen during the Recess of the Senate, by granting Commissions which shall expire at the End of their next Session.

Section. 3.

He shall from time to time give to the Congress Information of the State of the Union, and recommend to their Consideration such Measures as he shall judge necessary and expedient; he may, on extraordinary Occasions, convene both Houses, or either of them, and in Case of Disagreement between them, with Respect to the Time of Adjournment, he may adjourn them to such Time as he shall think proper; he shall receive Ambassadors and other public Ministers; he shall take Care that the Laws be faithfully executed, and shall Commission all the Officers of the United States.

Section. 4.

The President, Vice President and all civil Officers of the United States, shall be removed from Office on Impeachment for, and Conviction of, Treason, Bribery, or other high Crimes and Misdemeanors.

ARTICLE. III

Section. 1.

The judicial Power of the United States shall be vested in one supreme Court, and in such inferior Courts as the Congress may from time to time ordain and establish. The Judges, both of the supreme and inferior Courts, shall hold their Offices during good Behaviour, and shall, at stated Times, receive for their Services a Compensation, which shall not be diminished during their Continuance in Office.

Section. 2.

The judicial Power shall extend to all Cases, in Law and Equity, arising under this Constitution, the Laws of the United States, and Treaties made, or which shall be made, under their Authority; –– to all Cases affecting Ambassadors, other public Ministers and Consuls; –– to all Cases of admiralty and maritime Jurisdiction; –– to Controversies to which the United States shall be a Party; –– to Controversies between two or more States; –– <u>between a State and Citizens of another State,</u>—between Citizens of different States, –– between Citizens of the same State claiming Lands under Grants of different States, and between a State, or the Citizens thereof, and foreign States, Citizens or Subjects.

In all Cases affecting Ambassadors, other public Ministers and Consuls, and those in which a State shall be Party, the supreme Court shall have original Jurisdiction. In all the other Cases before mentioned, the supreme Court shall have appellate Jurisdiction, both as to Law and Fact, with such Exceptions, and under such Regulations as the Congress shall make.

The Trial of all Crimes, except in Cases of Impeachment, shall be by Jury; and such Trial shall be held in the State where the said Crimes shall have been committed; but when not committed within any State, the Trial shall be at such Place or Places as the Congress may by Law have directed.

Section. 3.

Treason against the United States, shall consist only in levying War against them, or in adhering to their Enemies, giving them Aid and Comfort. No Person shall be convicted of Treason unless on the Testimony of two Witnesses to the same overt Act, or on Confession in open Court.

The Congress shall have Power to declare the Punishment of Treason, but no Attainder of Treason shall work Corruption of Blood, or Forfeiture except during the Life of the Person attained.

ARTICLE. IV

Section. 1.

Full Faith and Credit shall be given in each State to the public Acts, Records, and judicial Proceedings of every other State. And the Congress may by general Laws prescribe the Manner in which such Acts, Records and Proceedings shall be proved, and the Effect thereof.

Section. 2.

The Citizens of each State shall be entitled to all Privileges and Immunities of Citizens in the several States.

A Person charged in any State with Treason, Felony, or other Crime, who shall flee from Justice, and be found in another State, shall on Demand of the executive Authority of the State from which he fled, be delivered up, to be removed to the State having Jurisdiction of the Crime.

No Person held to Service or Labour in one State, under the Laws thereof, escaping into another, shall, in Consequence of any Law or Regulation therein, be discharged from such Service or Labour, but shall be delivered up on Claim of the Party to whom such Service or Labour may be due.

Section. 3.

New States may be admitted by the Congress into this Union; but no new State shall be formed or erected within the Jurisdiction of any other State; nor any State be formed by the Junction of two or more States, or Parts of States, without the Consent of the Legislatures of the States concerned as well as of the Congress.

The Congress shall have Power to dispose of and make all needful Rules and Regulations respecting the Territory or other Property belonging to the United States; and nothing in this Constitution shall be so construed as to Prejudice any Claims of the United States, or of any particular State.

Section. 4.

The United States shall guarantee to every State in this Union a Republican Form of Government, and shall protect each of them against Invasion; and on Application of the Legislature, or of the Executive (when the Legislature cannot be convened), against domestic Violence.

ARTICLE. V

The Congress, whenever two thirds of both Houses shall deem it necessary, shall propose Amendments to this Constitution, or, on the Application of the Legislatures of two thirds of the several States, shall call a Convention for proposing Amendments, which, in either Case, shall be valid to all Intents and Purposes, as Part of this Constitution, when ratified by the Legislatures of three fourths of the several States, or by Conventions in three fourths thereof, as the one or the other Mode of Ratification may be proposed by the Congress; Provided that no Amendment which may be made prior to the Year One thousand eight hundred and eight shall in any Manner affect the first and fourth Clauses in the Ninth Section of the first Article; and that no State, without its Consent, shall be deprived of its equal Suffrage in the Senate.

ARTICLE. VI

All Debts contracted and Engagements entered into, before the Adoption of this Constitution, shall be as valid against the United States under this Constitution, as under the Confederation.

This Constitution, and the Laws of the United States which shall be made in Pursuance thereof; and all Treaties made, or which shall be made, under the Authority of the United States, shall be the supreme Law of the Land; and the Judges in every State shall be bound thereby, any Thing in the Constitution or Laws of any State to the Contrary notwithstanding.

The Senators and Representatives before mentioned, and the Members of the several State Legislatures, and all executive and judicial Officers, both of the United States and of the several States, shall be bound by Oath or Affirmation, to support this Constitution; but no religious Test shall ever be required as a Qualification to any Office or public Trust under the United States.

ARTICLE. VII

The Ratification of the Conventions of nine States, shall be sufficient for the Establishment of this Constitution between the States so ratifying the Same.

The Word, "the," being interlined between the seventh and eighth Lines of the first Page, the Word "Thirty" being partly written on an Erazure in the fifteenth Line of the first Page, The Words "is tried" being interlined between the thirty second and thirty third Lines of the first Page and the Word "the" being interlined between the forty third and forty fourth Lines of the second Page.

Attest William Jackson Secretary

Done in Convention by the Unanimous Consent of the States present the Seventeenth Day of September in the Year of our Lord one thousand seven hundred and Eighty seven and of the Independence of the United States of America the Twelfth In witness whereof We have hereunto subscribed our Names,

G°. Washington
Presidt and deputy from Virginia

LESSON TEN

THE BILL OF RIGHTS

Bill of Rights

(December 15, 1791)

United States Congress

▌The History[11]*

In the United States, the Bill of Rights is the name by which the first ten amendments to the United States Constitution are known. They were introduced by James Madison to the First United States Congress in 1789 as a series of articles, and came into effect on December 15, 1791, when they had been ratified by three-fourths of the States. Thomas Jefferson was a proponent of the Bill of Rights.

The Bill of Rights prohibits Congress from making any law respecting an establishment of religion or prohibiting the free exercise thereof, forbids infringement of "...the right of the people to keep and bear Arms...," and prohibits the federal government from depriving any person of life, liberty, or property, without due process of law. In federal criminal cases, it requires indictment by grand jury for any capital or "infamous crime," guarantees a speedy public trial with an impartial jury composed of members of the state or judicial district in which the crime occurred, and prohibits double jeopardy. In addition, the Bill of Rights states that "the enumeration in the Constitution, of certain rights, shall not be construed to deny or disparage others retained by the people," and reserves all powers not granted to the federal government to the citizenry or States. Most of these restrictions were later applied to the states by a series of decisions applying the due process clause of the Fourteenth Amendment, which was ratified in 1868, after the American Civil War.

Madison proposed the Bill of Rights while ideological conflict between Federalists and anti–Federalists, dating from the 1787 Philadelphia Convention, threatened the overall ratification of the new national Constitution. It largely responded to the Constitution's influential opponents, including prominent Founding Fathers, who argued that the Constitution should not be ratified because it failed to protect the basic principles of human liberty. The Bill was influenced by George Mason's 1776 Virginia Declaration of Rights, the 1689 English Bill of Rights, works of the Age of Enlightenment pertaining to natural rights, and earlier English political documents such as Magna Carta (1215).

Two additional articles were proposed to the States; only the final ten articles were ratified quickly and correspond to the First through Tenth Amendments to the Constitution. The first Article, dealing with the number and apportionment of U.S. Representatives, never became

---

[11] *Originally published as "United States Bill of Rights," *Wikipedia*, Wikimedia Foundation, Inc., San Francisco, California, November 2009. For additional information see "Bill of Rights," *The Charters of Freedom*, U.S. National Archives and Records Administration, College Park, Maryland, 2004. This agency is listed in the *National Resource Directory* section of this volume.

part of the Constitution. The second Article, limiting the ability of Congress to increase the salaries of its members, was ratified two centuries later as the 27th Amendment. Though they are incorporated into the document known as the "Bill of Rights," neither article establishes a right as that term is used today. For that reason, and also because the term had been applied to the first ten amendments long before the 27th Amendment was ratified, the term "Bill of Rights" in modern U.S. usage means only the ten amendments ratified in 1791.

The Bill of Rights plays a central role in American law and government, and remains a fundamental symbol of the freedoms and culture of the nation. One of the original fourteen copies of the Bill of Rights is on public display at the National Archives in Washington, D.C.

The Document

Bill of Rights

The Preamble to The Bill of Rights
Congress of the United States begun and held at the City of New York, on Wednesday the fourth of March, one thousand seven hundred and eighty nine.

THE Conventions of a number of the States, having at the time of their adopting the Constitution, expressed a desire, in order to prevent misconstruction or abuse of its powers, that further declaratory and restrictive clauses should be added. And as extending the ground of public confidence in the Government, will best ensure the beneficent ends of its institution.

RESOLVED by the Senate and House of Representatives of the United States of America, in Congress assembled, two thirds of both Houses concurring, that the following Articles be proposed to the Legislatures of the several States, as amendments to the Constitution of the United States, all, or any of which Articles, when ratified by three fourths of the said Legislatures, to be valid to all intents and purposes, as part of the said Constitution; viz.

ARTICLES in addition to, and Amendment of the Constitution of the United States of America, proposed by Congress, and ratified by the Legislatures of the several States, pursuant to the fifth Article of the original Constitution.

AMENDMENT I

Congress shall make no law respecting an establishment of religion, or prohibiting the free exercise thereof; or abridging the freedom of speech, or of the press; or the right of the people peaceably to assemble, and to petition the Government for a redress of grievances.

AMENDMENT II

A well-regulated militia, being necessary to the security of a free State, the right of the people to keep and bear arms, shall not be infringed.

AMENDMENT III

No soldier shall, in time of peace be quartered in any house, without the consent of the owner, nor in time of war, but in a manner to be prescribed by law.

AMENDMENT IV

The right of the people to be secure in their persons, houses, papers, and effects, against unreasonable searches and seizures, shall not be violated, and no warrants shall issue, but upon probable cause, supported by oath or affirmation, and particularly describing the place to be searched, and the persons or things to be seized.

AMENDMENT V

No person shall be held to answer for a capital, or otherwise infamous crime, unless on a presentment or indictment of a Grand Jury, except in cases arising in the land or naval forces, or in the militia, when in actual service in time of war or public danger; nor shall any person be subject for the same offense to be twice put in jeopardy of life or limb; nor shall be compelled in any criminal case to be a witness against himself, nor be deprived of life, liberty, or property, without due process of law; nor shall private property be taken for public use without just compensation.

AMENDMENT VI

In all criminal prosecutions, the accused shall enjoy the right to a speedy and public trial, by an impartial jury of the State and district wherein the crime shall have been committed, which district shall have been previously ascertained by law, and to be informed of the nature and cause of the accusation; to be confronted with the witnesses against him; to have compulsory process for obtaining witnesses in his favor, and to have the assistance of counsel for his defense.

AMENDMENT VII

In suits at common law, where the value in controversy shall exceed twenty dollars, the right of trial by jury shall be preserved, and no fact tried by a jury shall be otherwise reexamined in any court of the United States, than according to the rules of the common law.

AMENDMENT VIII

Excessive bail shall not be required, nor excessive fines imposed, nor cruel and unusual punishments inflicted.

AMENDMENT IX

The enumeration in the Constitution, of certain rights, shall not be construed to deny or disparage others retained by the people.

AMENDMENT X

The powers not delegated to the United States by the Constitution, nor prohibited by it to the States, are reserved to the States respectively, or to the people.

NOTE

The capitalization and punctuation in this version is from the enrolled original of the Joint Resolution of Congress proposing the Bill of Rights, which is on permanent display in the Rotunda of the National Archives Building, Washington, D.C. The above text is a transcription of the first ten amendments to the Constitution in their original form.

LESSON ELEVEN

OTHER AMENDMENTS TO THE CONSTITUTION
OF THE UNITED STATES

Other Amendments to the Constitution of the United States

(February 7, 1795, to May 7, 1992)

United States Congress

| The History[12]*

The authority to amend the Constitution of the United States is derived from Article V of the Constitution. After Congress proposes an amendment, the Archivist of the United States, who heads the National Archives and Records Administration (NARA), is charged with responsibility for administering the ratification process under the provisions of the United States Code (USC).

The Archivist has delegated many of the ministerial duties associated with this function to the Director of the Federal Register. Neither Article V of the Constitution nor section 106b describe the ratification process in detail. The Archivist and the Director of the Federal Register follow procedures and customs established by the Secretary of State, who performed these duties until 1950, and the Administrator of General Services, who served in this capacity until NARA assumed responsibility as an independent agency in 1985.

The Constitution provides that an amendment may be proposed either by the Congress with a two-thirds majority vote in both the House of Representatives and the Senate or by a constitutional convention called for by two-thirds of the State legislatures. None of the 27 amendments of the Constitution have been proposed by constitutional convention. The Congress proposes an amendment in the form of a joint resolution. Since the President does not have a constitutional role in the amendment process, the joint resolution does not go to the White House for signature or approval. The original document is forwarded directly to NARA's Office of the Federal Register (OFR) for processing and publication. The OFR adds legislative history notes to the joint resolution and publishes it in slip law format. The OFR also assembles an information package for the States which includes formal "red-line" copies of the joint resolution, copies of the joint resolution in slip law format, and the statutory procedure for ratification under 1 U.S.C. 106b.

The Archivist submits the proposed amendment to the Senate for their consideration by sending a letter of notification to each Governor along with the informational material prepared by the OFR. The Governors then formally submit the amendment to their State legislatures. In the past, some State legislatures have not waited to receive official notice before taking action on a proposed amendment. When a State ratifies a proposed amendment, it sends the Archivist an original or certified copy of the State action, which is immediately conveyed to the Director of the Federal Register. The OFR examines ratification documents for facial legal sufficiency and an

---

[12] *Originally published as "The Constitutional Amendment Process," *The Federal Register*, The National Archives, U.S. National Archives and Records Administration, College Park, Maryland, 2008. For additional information see "The Constitutional Amendment Process, *The Federal Register*, U.S. National Archives and Records Administration, College Park, Maryland, 2008. This agency is listed in the *National Resource Directory* section of this volume.

authenticating signature. If the documents are found to be in good order, the Director acknowledges receipt and maintains custody of them. The OFR retains these documents until an amendment is adopted or fails, and then transfers the records to the National Archives for preservation.

A proposed amendment becomes part of the Constitution as soon as it is ratified by three-fourths of the States (38 of 50 States). When the OFR verifies that it has received the required number of authenticated ratification documents, it drafts a formal proclamation for the Archivist to certify that the amendment is valid and has become part of the Constitution. This certification is published in the Federal Register and U.S. Statutes at Large and serves as official notice to the Congress and to the Nation that the amendment process has been completed.

In a few instances, States have sent official documents to NARA to record the rejection of an amendment or the rescission of a prior ratification. The Archivist does not make any substantive determinations as to the validity of State ratification actions, but it has been established that the Archivist's certification of the facial legal sufficiency of ratification documents is final and conclusive.

In recent history, the signing of the certification has become a ceremonial function attended by various dignitaries, which may include the President. President Johnson signed the certifications for the 24th and 25th Amendments as a witness, and President Nixon similarly witnessed the certification of the 26th Amendment along with three young scholars. On May 18, 1992, the Archivist performed the duties of the certifying official for the first time to recognize the ratification of the 27th Amendment, and the Director of the Federal Register signed the certification as a witness.

The Document

Other Amendments of the Constitution of the United States (Amendments XI to XXVII)

Constitutional Amendments 1–10 make up what is known as The Bill of Rights. Amendments 11–27 are given below.

Amendment XI

Note: Article III, section 2, of the Constitution was modified by the 11th amendment.
Passed by Congress March 4, 1794. Ratified February 7, 1795.
The Judicial power of the United States shall not be construed to extend to any suit in law or equity, commenced or prosecuted against one of the United States by citizens of another State, or by Citizens or Subjects of any Foreign State.

Amendment XII

Note: A portion of Article II, section 1 of the Constitution was superseded by the 12th amendment.
Passed by Congress December 9, 1803. Ratified July 27, 1804.

The Electors shall meet in their respective States and vote by ballot for President and Vice-President, one of whom, at least, shall not be an inhabitant of the same state with themselves; they shall name in their ballots the person voted for as President, and in distinct ballots the person voted for as Vice-President, and of the number of votes for each, which lists they shall sign and certify, and transmit sealed to the seat of the Government of the United States, directed to the President of the Senate; the President of the Senate shall, in the presence of the Senate and House of Representatives, open all the certificates and the votes shall then be counted; —— The person having the greatest number of votes for President, shall be the President, if such number be a majority of the whole number of Electors appointed; and if no person have such majority, then from the persons having the highest numbers not exceeding three on the list of those voted for as President, the House of Representatives shall choose immediately, by ballot, the President. But in choosing the President, the votes shall be taken by States, the representation from each State having one vote; a quorum for this purpose shall consist of a member or members from two-thirds of the States, and a majority of all the States shall be necessary to a choice. [And if the House of Representatives shall not choose a President whenever the right of choice shall devolve upon them, before the fourth day of March next following, then the Vice-President shall act as President, as in case of the death or other constitutional disability of the President. ——][13*] The person having the greatest number of votes as Vice-President, shall be the Vice-President, if such numbers be a majority of the whole number of electors appointed, and if no person have a majority, then from the two highest numbers on the list, the Senate shall choose the Vice-President; a quorum for the purpose shall consist of two-thirds of the whole number of Senators, and a majority of the whole number shall be necessary to a choice. But no person constitutionally ineligible to the office of President shall be eligible to that of Vice-President of the United States.

Amendment XIII

Note: A portion of Article IV, section 2, of the Constitution was superseded by the 13th Amendment.
Passed by Congress January 31, 1865. Ratified December 6, 1865.

Section 1.

Neither slavery nor involuntary servitude, except as a punishment for crime whereof the party shall have been duly convicted, shall exist within the United States, or any place subject to their jurisdiction.

Section 2.

Congress shall have power to enforce this article by appropriate legislation.

---

[13] * Superseded by section 3 of the 20th amendment.

Amendment XIV

Note: Article I, section 2, of the Constitution was modified by section 2 of the 14th amendment. *Passed by Congress June 13, 1866. Ratified July 9, 1868.*

Section 1.

All persons born or naturalized in the United States, and subject to the jurisdiction thereof, are citizens of the United States and of the State wherein they reside. No State shall make or enforce any law which shall abridge the privileges or immunities of citizens of the United States; nor shall any State deprive any person of life, liberty, or property, without due process of law; nor to deny to any person within its jurisdiction the equal protection of the laws.

Section 2.

Representatives shall be apportioned among the several States according to their respective numbers, counting the whole number of persons in each State, excluding Indians not taxed. But when the right to vote at any election for the choice of Electors for President and Vice-President of the United States, Representatives in Congress, the executive and judicial officers of a State, or the members of the legislature thereof, is denied to any of the male inhabitants of such State, being twenty-one years of age,[14*] and citizens of the United States, or in any way abridged, except for participation in rebellion, or other crime, the basis of representation therein shall be reduced in the proportion which the number of such male citizens shall bear to the whole number of male citizens twenty-one years of age in such State.

Section 3.

No person shall be a Senator or Representative in Congress, or Elector of President and Vice-President, or hold any office, civil or military, under the United States, or under any State, who, having previously taken an oath, as a member of Congress, or as an officer of the United States, or as a member of any State Legislature, or as an executive or judicial officer of any State, to support the Constitution of the United States, shall have engaged in insurrection or rebellion against the same, or given aid or comfort to the enemies thereof. But Congress may by a vote of two-thirds of each House, remove such disability.

Section 4.

The validity of the public debt of the United States, authorized by law, including debts incurred for payment of pensions and bounties for services in suppressing insurrection or rebellion, shall not be questioned. But neither the United States nor any State shall assume or pay any debt or obligation incurred in aid of insurrection or rebellion against the United States, or any claim

---

[14] * *Changed by section 1 of the 26th amendment.*

for the loss or emancipation of any slave; but all such debts, obligations and claims shall be held illegal and void.

Section 5.

The Congress shall have the power to enforce, by appropriate legislation, the provisions of this article.

AMENDMENT XV

Passed by Congress February 26, 1869. Ratified February 3, 1870.

Section 1.

The right of citizens of the United States to vote shall not be denied or abridged by the United States or by any State on account of race, color, or previous condition of servitude.

Section 2.

The Congress shall have the power to enforce this article by appropriate legislation.

AMENDMENT XVI

Note: Article I, section 3, of the Constitution was modified by the 17th amendment.
Passed by Congress July 2, 1909. Ratified February 3, 1913.
The Congress shall have power to lay and collect taxes on incomes, from whatever sources derived, without apportionment among the several States, and without regard to any census or enumeration.

AMENDMENT XVII

Note: Article I, section 3, of the Constitution was modified by the 17th amendment.
Passed by Congress May 13, 1912. Ratified April 8, 1913.
The Senate of the United States shall be composed of two Senators from each State, elected by the people thereof, for six years; and each Senator shall have one vote. The electors in each State shall have the qualifications requisite for electors of the most numerous branch of the State Legislatures.

When vacancies happen in the representation of any State in the Senate, the executive authority of such State shall issue writs of election to fill such vacancies: Provided, That the Legislature of any State may empower the Executive thereof to make temporary appointments until the people fill the vacancies by election as the Legislature may direct.

This amendment shall not be so construed as to affect the election or term of any Senator chosen before it becomes valid as part of the Constitution.

Amendment XVIII

Passed by Congress December 18, 1917. Ratified January 16, 1919. Repealed by amendment 21.

Section 1.

After one year from the ratification of this article the manufacture, sale, or transportation of intoxicating liquors within, the importation thereof into, or the exportation thereof from the United States and all territory subject to the jurisdiction thereof for beverage purposes is hereby prohibited.

Section 2.

The Congress and the several States shall have concurrent power to enforce this article by appropriate legislation.

Section 3.

This article shall be inoperative unless it shall have been ratified as an amendment to the Constitution by the Legislatures of the several States, as provided in the Constitution, within seven years from the date of the submission hereof to the States by the Congress.

Amendment XIX

Passed by Congress June 4, 1919. Ratified August 18, 1920.
The right of citizens of the United States to vote shall not be denied or abridged by the United States or by any State on account of sex.
Congress shall have power to enforce this article by appropriate legislation.

Amendment XX

Note: Article I, section 4, of the Constitution was modified by section 2 of this amendment. In addition, a portion of the 12th amendment was superseded by section 3.
Passed by Congress March 2, 1932. Ratified January 23, 1933.

Section 1.

The terms of the President and the Vice-President shall end at noon on the 20th day of January, and the terms of Senators and Representatives at noon on the 3rd day of January, of the years in which such terms would have ended if this article had not been ratified; and the terms of their successors shall then begin.

Section 2.

The Congress shall assemble at least once in every year, and such meeting shall begin at noon on the 3rd day of January, unless they shall by law appoint a different day.

Section 3.

If, at the time fixed for the beginning of the term of the President, the President elect shall have died, the Vice-President elect shall become President. If a President shall not have been chosen before the time fixed for the beginning of his term, or if the President elect shall have failed to qualify, then the Vice-President elect shall act as President until a President shall have qualified; and the Congress may by law provide for the case wherein neither a President elect nor a Vice-President shall have qualified, declaring who shall then act as President, or the manner in which one who is to act shall be selected, and such person shall act accordingly until a President or Vice-President shall have qualified.

Section 4.

The Congress may by law provide for the case of the death of any of the persons from whom the House of representatives may choose a President whenever the right of choice shall have devolved upon them, and for the case of the death of any of the persons from whom the Senate may choose a Vice-President whenever the right of choice shall have devolved upon them.

Section 5.

Sections 1 and 2 shall take effect on the 15th day of October following the ratification of this article (October 1933).

Section 6.

This article shall be inoperative unless it shall have been ratified as an amendment to the Constitution by the Legislatures of three-fourths of the several States within seven years from the date of its submission.

Amendment XXI

Passed by Congress February 20, 1933. Ratified December 5, 1933.

Section 1.

The Eighteenth article of amendment to the Constitution of the United States is hereby repealed.

Section 2.

The transportation or importation into any State, Territory, or Possession of the United States for delivery or use therein of intoxicating liquors, in violation of the laws thereof, is hereby prohibited.

Section 3.

This article shall be inoperative unless it shall have been ratified as an amendment to the Constitution by conventions in the several States, as provided in the Constitution, within seven years from the date of the submission hereof to the States by the Congress.

AMENDMENT XXII

Passed by Congress March 21, 1947. Ratified February 27, 1951.

Section 1.

No person shall be elected to the office of the President more than twice, and no person who has held the office of President, or acted as President, for more that two years of a term to which some other person was elected President shall be elected to the office of President more than once.

Section 2.

This article shall be inoperative unless it shall have been ratified as an amendment to the Constitution by the Legislatures of three-fourths of the several States within seven years from the date of its submission to the States by the Congress.

AMENDMENT XXIII

Passed by Congress June 16, 1960. Ratified March 29, 1961.

Section 1.

The District constituting the seat of Government of the United States shall appoint in such manner as Congress may direct:
A number of electors of President and Vice President equal to the whole number of Senators and Representatives in Congress to which the District would be entitled if it were a State, but in no event more than the least populous State; they shall be in addition to those appointed by the States, but they shall be considered, for the purposes of the election of President and Vice President, to be electors appointed by a State; and they shall meet in the District and perform such duties as provided by the twelfth article of amendment.

Section 2.

The Congress shall have power to enforce this article by appropriate legislation.

AMENDMENT XXIV

Passed by Congress August 27, 1962. Ratified January 23, 1964.

Section 1.

The right of citizens of the United States to vote in any primary or other election for President or Vice President, for electors for President or Vice President, or for Senator or Representative in Congress, shall not be denied or abridged by the United States or any State by reason of failure to pay poll tax or any other tax.

Section 2.

Congress shall have power to enforce this article by appropriate legislation.

AMENDMENT XXV

Note: Article II, section 1, of the Constitution was affected by the 25th amendment.
Passed by Congress July 6, 1965. Ratified February 10, 1967.

Section 1.

In case of the removal of the President from office or of his death or resignation, the Vice President shall become President.

Section 2.

Whenever there is a vacancy in the office of the Vice President, the President shall nominate a Vice President who shall take the office upon confirmation by a majority vote of both houses of Congress.

Section 3.

Whenever the President transmits to the President Pro tempore of the Senate and the Speaker of the House of Representatives his written declaration that he is unable to discharge the powers and duties of his office, and until he transmits to them a written declaration to the contrary, such powers and duties shall be discharged by the Vice President as Acting President.

Section 4.

Whenever the Vice President and a majority of either the principal officers of the executive departments or of such other body as Congress may by law provide, transmits to the President Pro tempore of the Senate and the Speaker of the House of Representatives their written declaration that the President is unable to discharge the powers and duties of his office, the Vice President shall immediately assume the powers and duties of the office as Acting President.

Thereafter, when the President transmits to the President Pro tempore of the Senate and the Speaker of the House of Representatives his written declaration that no inability exists, he shall resume the powers and duties of his office unless the Vice President and a majority of either the principal officers of the executive departments or of such other body as Congress may by law provide, transmits within four days to the President Pro tempore of the Senate and the Speaker of the House of Representatives their written declaration that the President is unable to discharge the powers and duties of his office. Thereupon Congress shall decide the issue, assembling within forty-eight hours for that purpose if not in session. If the Congress, within twenty-one days after receipt of the latter written declaration, or, if Congress is not in session within twenty-one days after Congress is required to assemble, determines by two-thirds vote of both houses that the President is unable to discharge the powers and duties of his office, the Vice President shall continue to discharge the same as Acting President; otherwise, the President shall resume the powers and duties of his office.

AMENDMENT XXVI

Note: Amendment 14, section 2, of the Constitution was modified by section 1 of the 26th amendment.
Passed by Congress March 23, 1971. Ratified June 30, 1971.

Section 1.

The right of citizens of the United States, who are 18 years of age or older, to vote shall not be denied or abridged by the United States or any state on account of age.

Section 2.

The Congress shall have power to enforce this article by appropriate legislation.

AMENDMENT XXVII

Originally proposed September 25, 1789. Ratified May 7, 1992.
No law, varying the compensation for services of the Senators and Representatives, shall take effect, until an election of Representatives shall have intervened.

LESSON TWELVE

THE CIVIL RIGHTS ACT

Civil Rights Act

(July 2, 1964)

United States Congress

▌The History[15*]

In the 1960s, Americans who knew only the potential of "equal protection of the laws" expected by the president, the Congress, and the courts to fulfill the promise of the 14th Amendment. In response, all three branches of the federal government — as well as the public at large — debated a fundamental constitutional question: Does the Constitution's prohibition of denying equal protection always ban the use of racial, ethnic, or gender criteria in an attempt to bring social justice and social benefits?

In 1964 Congress passed Public Law 82-352 (78 Stat. 241). The provisions of this civil rights act forbade discrimination on the basis of sex as well as race in hiring, promoting, and firing. The word "sex" was added at the last moment. According to the *West Encyclopedia of American Law*, Representative Howard W. Smith (D-VA) added the word. His critics argued that Smith, a conservative Southern opponent of federal civil rights, did so to kill the entire bill. Smith, however, argued that he had amended the bill in keeping with his support of Alice Paul and the National Women's Party with whom he had been working. Martha W. Griffiths (D-MI) led the effort to keep the word "sex" in the bill.

In the final legislation, Section 703 (a) made it unlawful for an employer to "fail or refuse to hire or to discharge any individual, or otherwise to discriminate against any individual with respect to his compensation, terms, conditions or privileges or employment, because of such individual's race, color, religion, sex, or national origin." The final bill also allowed sex to be a consideration when sex is a bona fide occupational qualification for the job. Title VII of the act created the Equal Employment Opportunity Commission (EEOC) to implement the law.

Subsequent legislation expanded the role of the EEOC. Today, according to the *U.S. Government Manual of 1998–99*, the EEOC enforces laws that prohibit discrimination based on race, color, religion, sex, national origin, disability, or age in hiring, promoting, firing, setting wages, testing, training, apprenticeship, and all other terms and conditions of employment. Race, color, sex, creed, and age are not protected classes. The proposal to add each group to

---

[15] * Originally published as "Teaching With Documents: The Civil Rights Act of 1964 and the Equal Opportunity Employment Commission," *Educators and Students Report*, The National Archives, U.S. National Archives and Records Administration, College Park, Maryland, 2008. For additional information see "Teaching with Documents: The Civil Rights Act of 1964 and the Equal Employment Opportunity Commission," *Educators and Students Report*, U.S. National Archives and Records Administration, College Park, Maryland, 2008. This agency is listed in the *National Resource Directory* section of this volume.

protected-class status unleashed furious debate. But no words stimulate the passion of the debate more than "affirmative action."

As West defines the term, affirmative action "refers to both mandatory and voluntary programs intended to affirm the civil rights of designated classes of individuals by taking positive action to protect them" from discrimination. The issue for most Americans is fairness: Should the equal protection clause of the 14th Amendment be used to advance the liberty of one class of individuals for good reasons when that action may infringe on the liberty of another?

The EEOC, as an independent regulatory body, plays a major role in dealing with this issue. Since its creation in 1964, Congress has gradually extended EEOC powers to include investigatory authority, creating conciliation programs, filing lawsuits, and conducting voluntary assistance programs. While the Civil Rights Act of 1964 did not mention the words affirmative action, it did authorize the bureaucracy to make rules to help end discrimination. The EEOC has done so.

Today the regulatory authority of the EEOC includes enforcing a range of federal statutes prohibiting employment discrimination. According to the EEOC's own Web site, these include Title VII of the Civil Rights Act of 1964 that prohibits employment discrimination on the basis of race, color, religion, sex, or national origin; the Age Discrimination in Employment Act of 1967, and its amendments, that prohibits employment discrimination against individuals 40 years of age or older; the Equal Pay Act of 1963 that prohibits discrimination on the basis of gender in compensation for substantially similar work under similar conditions; Title I of the Americans with Disabilities Act of 1990 that prohibits employment discrimination on the basis of disability in both the public and private sector, excluding the federal government; the Civil Rights Act of 1991 that provides for monetary damages in case of intentional discrimination; and Section 501 of the Rehabilitation Act of 1973, as amended, that prohibits employment discrimination against federal employees with disabilities. Title IX of the Education Act of 1972 forbade gender discrimination in education programs, including athletics, that received federal dollars. In the late 1970s Congress passed the Pregnancy Discrimination Act. This made it illegal for employers to exclude pregnancy and childbirth from their sick leave and health benefits plans.

Presidents also weighed in, employing a series of executive orders. President Lyndon B. Johnson ordered all executive agencies to require federal contractors to "take affirmative action to ensure that applicants are employed and that employees are treated during employment without regard to race, color, religion, sex, or national origin." This marked the first use of the phrase "affirmative action." In 1969 an executive order required that every level of federal service offer equal opportunities for women and established a program to implement that action. President Richard Nixon's Department of Labor adopted a plan requiring federal contractors to assess their employees to identify gender and race and to set goals to end any under-representation of women and minorities. By the 1990s Democratic and Republican administrations had taken a variety of actions that resulted in 160 different affirmative action federal programs. State and local governments were following suit.

The courts also addressed affirmative action. In addition to dealing with race, color, creed, and age, from the 1970s forward, the court dealt with gender questions. It voided arbitrary weight and height requirements (*Dothard v. Rawlinson*), erased mandatory pregnancy leaves (*Cleveland*

Board of Education v. LaFleur), allowed public employers to use carefully constructed affirmative action plans to remedy specific past discrimination that resulted in women and minorities being under-represented in the workplace (*Johnson v. Transportation Agency, Santa Clara County*), and upheld state and local laws prohibiting gender discrimination.

By the late 1970s all branches of the federal government and most state governments had taken at least some action to fulfill the promise of equal protection under the law. The EEOC served as the agent of implementation and complaint. Its activism divided liberals and conservatives, illuminating their differing views about the proper scope of government. In general, the political liberals embraced the creation of the EEOC as the birth of a federal regulatory authority that could promote the goal of equality by designing policies to help the historically disadvantaged, including women and minorities. In contrast, political conservatives saw the EEOC as a violation of their belief in fewer government regulations and fewer federal policies. To them, creating a strong economy, free from government intervention, would produce gains that would benefit the historically disadvantaged. Even the nonideological segment of the American population asked: What should government do, if anything, to ensure equal protection under the law?

In fiscal year 1997, the EEOC collected $111 million dollars in financial benefits for people who filed claims of discrimination. Its recent successful efforts include a $34 million settlement in a sexual harassment case with Mitsubishi Motor Manufacturing of America, resulting in the company's adoption of changes to its sexual harassment prevention policy. Working with state and local programs, the EEOC processes 48,000 claims annually.

The Document

Civil Rights Act

To enforce the constitutional right to vote, to confer jurisdiction upon the district courts of the United States to provide injunctive relief against discrimination in public accommodations, to authorize the Attorney General to institute suits to protect constitutional rights in public facilities and public education, to extend the Commission on Civil Rights, to prevent discrimination in federally assisted programs, to establish a Commission on Equal Employment Opportunity, and for other purposes.

Be it enacted by the Senate and House of Representatives of the United States of America in Congress assembled, That this Act may be cited as the "Civil Rights Act of 1964."

Title I –– Voting Rights

SEC. 101. Section 2004 of the Revised Statutes (42 U.S.C. 1971), as amended by section 131 of the Civil Rights Act of 1957 (71 Stat. 637), and as further amended by section 601 of the Civil Rights Act of 1960 (74 Stat. 90), is further amended as follows:

(a) Insert "1" after "(a)" in subsection (a) and add at the end of subsection (a) the following new paragraphs:

"(2) No person acting under color of law shall ––

"(A) in determining whether any individual is qualified under State law or laws to vote in any Federal election, apply any standard, practice, or procedure different from the standards, practices, or procedures applied under such law or laws to other individuals within the same county, parish, or similar political subdivision who have been found by State officials to be qualified to vote;

"(B) deny the right of any individual to vote in any Federal election because of an error or omission on any record or paper relating to any application, registration, or other act requisite to voting, if such error or omission is not material in determining whether such individual is qualified under State law to vote in such election; or

"(C) employ any literacy test as a qualification for voting in any Federal election unless (i) such test is administered to each individual and is conducted wholly in writing, and (ii) a certified copy of the test and of the answers given by the individual is furnished to him within twenty-five days of the submission of his request made within the period of time during which records and papers are required to be retained and preserved pursuant to title III of the Civil Rights Act of 1960 (42 U.S.C. 1974 –– 74e; 74 Stat. 88): Provided, however, That the Attorney General may enter into agreements with appropriate State or local authorities that preparation, conduct, and maintenance of such tests in accordance with the provisions of applicable State or local law, including such special provisions as are necessary in the preparation, conduct, and maintenance of such tests for persons who are blind or otherwise physically handicapped, meet the purposes of this subparagraph and constitute compliance therewith.

"(3) For purposes of this subsection ––

"(A) the term 'vote' shall have the same meaning as in subsection (e) of this section;

"(B) the phrase 'literacy test' includes any test of the ability to read, write, understand, or interpret any matter."

(b) Insert immediately following the period at the end of the first sentence of subsection (c) the following new sentence: "If in any such proceeding literacy is a relevant fact there shall be a rebuttable presumption that any person who has not been adjudged an incompetent and who has completed the sixth grade in a public school in, or a private school accredited by, any State or territory, the District of Columbia, or the Commonwealth of Puerto Rico where instruction is carried on predominantly in the English language, possesses sufficient literacy, comprehension, and intelligence to vote in any Federal election."

(c) Add the following subsection "(f)" and designate the present subsection "(f)" as subsection "(g)": "(f) When used in subsection (a) or (c) of this section, the words 'Federal election' shall mean any general, special, or primary election held solely or in part for the purpose of electing or selecting any candidate for the office of President, Vice President, presidential elector, Member of the Senate, or Member of the House of Representatives."

(d) Add the following subsection "(h)":

"(h) In any proceeding instituted by the United States in any district court of the United States under this section in which the Attorney General requests a finding of a pattern or practice of discrimination pursuant to subsection (e) of this section the Attorney General, at the time he files the complaint, or any defendant in the proceeding, within twenty days after service upon him of the complaint, may file with the clerk of such court a request that a court of three judges be convened to hear and determine the entire case. A copy of the request for a three-judge court shall be immediately furnished by such clerk to the chief judge of the circuit (or in his absence, the presiding circuit judge of the circuit) in which the case is pending. Upon receipt of the copy of such request it shall be the duty of the chief justice of the circuit or the presiding circuit judge, as the case may be, to designate immediately three judges in such circuit, of whom at least one shall be a circuit judge and another of whom shall be a district judge of the court in which the proceeding was instituted, to hear and determine such case, and it shall be the duty of the judges so designated to assign the case for hearing at the earliest practicable date, to participate in the hearing and determination thereof, and to cause the case to be in every way expedited.

An appeal from the final judgment of such court will lie to the Supreme Court.

"In any proceeding brought under subsection (c) of this section to enforce subsection (b) of this section, or in the event neither the Attorney General nor any defendant files a request for a three-judge court in any proceeding authorized by this subsection, it shall be the duty of the chief judge of the district (or in his absence, the acting chief judge) in which the case is pending immediately to designate a judge in such district to hear and determine the case. In the event that no judge in the district is available to hear and determine the case, the chief judge of the district, or the acting chief judge, as the case may be, shall certify this fact to the chief judge of the circuit (or, in his absence, the acting chief judge) who shall then designate a district or circuit judge of the circuit to hear and determine the case.

"It shall be the duty of the judge designated pursuant to this section to assign the case for hearing at the earliest practicable date and to cause the case to be in every way expedited."

Title II—Injunctive Relief Against Discrimination in Places of Public Accommodation

SEC. 201. (a) All persons shall be entitled to the full and equal enjoyment of the goods, services, facilities, and privileges, advantages, and accommodations of any place of public accommodation, as defined in this section, without discrimination or segregation on the ground of race, color, religion, or national origin.

(b) Each of the following establishments which serves the public is a place of public accommodation within the meaning of this title if its operations affect commerce, or if discrimination or segregation by it is supported by State action:

(1) any inn, hotel, motel, or other establishment which provides lodging to transient guests, other than an establishment located within a building which contains not more than five rooms for rent or hire and which is actually occupied by the proprietor of such establishment as his residence;

(2) any restaurant, cafeteria, lunchroom, lunch counter, soda fountain, or other facility principally engaged in selling food for consumption on the premises, including, but not limited to, any such facility located on the premises of any retail establishment; or any gasoline station;

(3) any motion picture house, theater, concert hall, sports arena, stadium or other place of exhibition or entertainment; and

(4) any establishment (A)(i) which is physically located within the premises of any establishment

otherwise covered by this subsection, or (ii) within the premises of which is physically located any such covered establishment, and (B) which holds itself out as serving patrons of such covered establishment.

(c) The operations of an establishment affect commerce within the meaning of this title if (1) it is one of the establishments described in paragraph (1) of subsection (b); (2) in the case of an establishment described in paragraph (2) of subsection (b), it serves or offers to serve interstate travelers or a substantial portion of the food which it serves, or gasoline or other products which it sells, has moved in commerce; (3) in the case of an establishment described in paragraph (3) of subsection (b), it customarily presents films, performances, athletic teams, exhibitions, or other sources of entertainment which move in commerce; and (4) in the case of an establishment described in paragraph (4) of subsection (b), it is physically located within the premises of, or there is physically located within its premises, an establishment the operations of which affect commerce within the meaning of this subsection. For purposes of this section, "commerce" means travel, trade, traffic, commerce, transportation, or communication among the several States, or between the District of Columbia and any State, or between any foreign country or any territory or possession and any State or the District of Columbia, or between points in the same State but through any other State or the District of Columbia or a foreign country.

(d) Discrimination or segregation by an establishment is supported by State action within the meaning of this title if such discrimination or segregation (1) is carried on under color of any law, statute, ordinance, or regulation; or (2) is carried on under color of any custom or usage required or enforced by officials of the State or political subdivision thereof; or (3) is required by action of the State or political subdivision thereof.

(e) The provisions of this title shall not apply to a private club or other establishment not in fact open to the public, except to the extent that the facilities of such establishment are made available to the customers or patrons of an establishment within the scope of subsection (b).

SEC. 202. All persons shall be entitled to be free, at any establishment or place, from discrimination or segregation of any kind on the ground of race, color, religion, or national origin, if such discrimination or segregation is or purports to be required by any law, statute, ordinance, regulation, rule, or order of a State or any agency or political subdivision thereof.

SEC. 203. No person shall (a) withhold, deny, or attempt to withhold or deny, or deprive or attempt to deprive, any person of any right or privilege secured by section 201 or 202, or (b) intimidate, threaten, or coerce, or attempt to intimidate, threaten, or coerce any person with the purpose of interfering with any right or privilege secured by section 201 or 202, or (c) punish or attempt to punish any person for exercising or attempting to exercise any right or privilege secured by section 201 or 202.

SEC. 204. (a) Whenever any person has engaged or there are reasonable grounds to believe that any person is about to engage in any act or practice prohibited by section 203, a civil action for preventive relief, including an application for a permanent or temporary injunction, restraining order, or other order, may be instituted by the person aggrieved and, upon timely application, the court may, in its discretion, permit the Attorney General to intervene in such civil action if he certifies that the case is of general public importance. Upon application by the complainant and in such circumstances as the court may deem just, the court may appoint an attorney for such complainant and may authorize the commencement of the civil action without the payment of fees, costs, or security.

(b) In any action commenced pursuant to this title, the court, in its discretion, may allow the prevailing party, other than the United States, a reasonable attorney's fee as part of the costs, and the United States shall be liable for costs the same as a private person.

(c) In the case of an alleged act or practice prohibited by this title which occurs in a State, or political subdivision of a State, which has a State or local law prohibiting such act or practice and establishing or authorizing a State or local authority to grant or seek relief from such practice or to institute criminal proceedings with respect thereto upon receiving notice thereof, no civil action may be brought under subsection (a) before the expiration of thirty days after written notice of such alleged act or practice has been given to the appropriate State or local authority by registered mail or in person, provided that the court may stay proceedings in such civil action pending the termination of State or local enforcement proceedings.

(d) In the case of an alleged act or practice prohibited by this title which occurs in a State, or political subdivision of a State, which has no State or local law prohibiting such act or practice, a civil action may be brought under subsection (a): Provided, That the court may refer the matter to the Community Relations Service established by title X of this Act for as long as the court believes there is a reasonable possibility of obtaining voluntary compliance, but for not more than sixty days: Provided further, That upon expiration of such sixty-day period, the court may extend such period for an additional period, not to exceed a cumulative total of one hundred and twenty days, if it believes there then exists a reasonable possibility of securing voluntary compliance.

SEC. 205. The Service is authorized to make a full investigation of any complaint referred to it by the court under section 204(d) and may hold such hearings with respect thereto as may be necessary. The Service shall conduct any hearings with respect to any such complaint in executive session, and shall not release any testimony given therein except by agreement of all parties involved in the complaint with the permission of the court, and the Service shall endeavor to bring about a voluntary settlement between the parties.

SEC. 206. (a) Whenever the Attorney General has reasonable cause to believe that any person or group of persons is engaged in a pattern or practice of resistance to the full enjoyment of any of the rights secured by this title, and that the pattern or practice is of such a nature and is intended to deny the full exercise of the rights herein described, the Attorney General may bring a civil action in the appropriate district court of the United States by filing with it a complaint (1) signed by him (or in his absence the Acting Attorney General), (2) setting forth facts pertaining to such pattern or practice, and (3) requesting such preventive relief, including an application for a permanent or temporary injunction, restraining order or other order against the person or persons responsible for such pattern or practice, as he deems necessary to insure the full enjoyment of the rights herein described.

(b) In any such proceeding the Attorney General may file with the clerk of such court a request that a court of three judges be convened to hear and determine the case. Such request by the Attorney General shall be accompanied by a certificate that, in his opinion, the case is of general public importance. A copy of the certificate and request for a three-judge court shall be immediately furnished by such clerk to the chief judge of the circuit (or in his absence, the presiding circuit judge of the circuit) in which the case is pending. Upon receipt of the copy of such request it shall be the duty of the chief judge of the circuit or the presiding circuit judge, as the case may be, to designate immediately three judges in such circuit, of whom at least one shall be a circuit judge and another of whom shall be a district judge of the court in which the proceeding was instituted, to hear and determine such case, and it shall be the duty of the judges so designated to assign the case for hearing at the earliest practicable date, to participate in the hearing and determination thereof, and to cause the case to be in every way expedited. An appeal from the final judgment of such court will lie to the Supreme Court.

In the event the Attorney General fails to file such a request in any such proceeding, it shall be the duty of the chief judge of the district (or in his absence, the acting chief judge) in which the case is pending immediately to designate a judge in such district to hear and determine the case. In the event that no judge in the district is available to hear and determine the case, the chief judge of the district, or the acting chief judge, as the case may be, shall certify this fact to the chief judge of the circuit (or in his absence, the acting chief judge) who shall then designate a district or circuit judge of the circuit to hear and determine the case.

It shall be the duty of the judge designated pursuant to this section to assign the case for hearing at the earliest practicable date and to cause the case to be in every way expedited.

SEC. 207. (a) The district courts of the United States shall have jurisdiction of proceedings instituted pursuant to this title and shall exercise the same without regard to whether the aggrieved party shall have exhausted any administrative or other remedies that may be provided by law.

(b) The remedies provided in this title shall be the exclusive means of enforcing the rights based on this title, but nothing in this title shall preclude any individual or any State or local agency from asserting any right based on any other Federal or State law not inconsistent with this title, including any statute or ordinance requiring nondiscrimination in public establishments or accommodations, or from pursuing any remedy, civil or criminal, which may be available for the vindication or enforcement of such right.

Title III –– Desegregation of Public Facilities

SEC. 301. (a) Whenever the Attorney General receives a complaint in writing signed by an individual to the effect that he is being deprived of or threatened with the loss of his right to the equal protection of the laws, on account of his race, color, religion, or national origin, by being denied equal utilization of any public facility which is owned, operated, or managed by or on behalf of any State or subdivision thereof, other than a public school or public college as defined in section 401 of title IV hereof, and the Attorney General believes the complaint is meritorious and certifies that the signer or signers of such complaint are unable, in his judgment, to initiate and maintain appropriate legal proceedings for relief and that the institution of an action will materially further the orderly progress of desegregation in public facilities, the Attorney General is authorized to institute for or in the name of the United States a civil action in any appropriate district court of the United States against such parties and for such relief as may be appropriate, and such court shall have and shall exercise jurisdiction of proceedings instituted pursuant to this section. The Attorney General may implead as defendants such additional parties as are or become necessary to the grant of effective relief hereunder.

(b) The Attorney General may deem a person or persons unable to initiate and maintain appropriate legal proceedings within the meaning of subsection

(a) of this section when such person or persons are unable, either directly or through other interested persons or organizations, to bear the expense of the litigation or to obtain effective legal representation; or whenever he is satisfied that the institution of such litigation would jeopardize the personal safety, employment, or economic standing of such person or persons, their families, or their property.

SEC. 302. In any action or proceeding under this title the United States shall be liable for costs, including a reasonable attorney's fee, the same as a private person.

SEC. 303. Nothing in this title shall affect adversely the right of any person to sue for or obtain relief in any court against discrimination in any facility covered by this title.

SEC. 304. A complaint as used in this title is a writing or document within the meaning of section 1001, title 18, United States Code.

TITLE IV –– DESEGREGATION OF PUBLIC EDUCATION

Definitions

SEC. 401. As used in this title ––

(a) "Commissioner" means the Commissioner of Education.

(b) "Desegregation" means the assignment of students to public schools and within such schools without regard to their race, color, religion, or national origin, but "desegregation" shall not mean the assignment of students to public schools in order to overcome racial imbalance.

(c) "Public school" means any elementary or secondary educational institution, and "public college" means any institution of higher education or any technical or vocational school above the secondary school level, provided that such public school or public college is operated by a State, subdivision of a State, or governmental agency within a State, or operated wholly or predominantly from or through the use of governmental funds or property, or funds or property derived from a governmental source.

(d) "School board" means any agency or agencies which administer a system of one or more public schools and any other agency which is responsible for the assignment of students to or within such system.

SURVEY AND REPORT OF EDUCATIONAL OPPORTUNITIES

SEC. 402. The Commissioner shall conduct a survey and make a report to the President and the Congress, within two years of the enactment of this title, concerning the lack of availability of equal educational opportunities for individuals by reason of race, color, religion, or national origin in public educational institutions at all levels in the United States, its territories and possessions, and the District of Columbia.

TECHNICAL ASSISTANCE

SEC. 403. The Commissioner is authorized, upon the application of any school board, State, municipality, school district, or other governmental unit legally responsible for operating a public school or schools, to render technical assistance to such applicant in the preparation, adoption, and implementation of plans for the desegregation of public schools. Such technical assistance may, among other activities, include making available to such agencies information regarding effective methods of coping with special educational problems occasioned by desegregation, and making available to such agencies personnel of the Office of Education or other persons specially equipped to advise and assist them in coping with such problems.

TRAINING INSTITUTES

SEC. 404. The Commissioner is authorized to arrange, through grants or contracts, with institutions of higher education for the operation of short-term or regular session institutes for special training designed to improve the ability of teachers, supervisors, counselors, and other elementary or secondary school personnel to deal effectively with special educational problems occasioned by desegregation. Individuals who attend such an institute on a full-time basis may be paid stipends for the period of their attendance at such institute in amounts specified by the Commissioner in regulations, including allowances for travel to attend such institute.

Grants

SEC. 405. (a) The Commissioner is authorized, upon application of a school board, to make grants to such board to pay, in whole or in part, the cost of ––

(1) giving to teachers and other school personnel inservice training in dealing with problems incident to desegregation, and

(2) employing specialists to advise in problems incident to desegregation.

(b) In determining whether to make a grant, and in fixing the amount thereof and the terms and conditions on which it will be made, the Commissioner shall take into consideration the amount available for grants under this section and the other applications which are pending before him; the financial condition of the applicant and the other resources available to it; the nature, extent, and gravity of its problems incident to desegregation; and such other factors as he finds relevant.

Payments

SEC. 406. Payments pursuant to a grant or contract under this title may be made (after necessary adjustments on account of previously made overpayments or underpayments) in advance or by way of reimbursement, and in such installments, as the Commissioner may determine.

Suits by the Attorney General

SEC. 407. (a) Whenever the Attorney General receives a complaint in writing —

(1) signed by a parent or group of parents to the effect that his or their minor children, as members of a class of persons similarly situated, are being deprived by a school board of the equal protection of the laws, or

(2) signed by an individual, or his parent, to the effect that he has been denied admission to or not permitted to continue in attendance at a public college by reason of race, color, religion, or national origin, and the Attorney General believes the complaint is meritorious and certifies that the signer or signers of such complaint are unable, in his judgment, to initiate and maintain appropriate legal proceedings for relief and that the institution of an action will materially further the orderly achievement of desegregation in public education, the Attorney General is authorized, after giving notice of such complaint to the appropriate school board or college authority and after certifying that he is satisfied that such board or authority has had a reasonable time to adjust the conditions alleged in such complaint, to institute for or in the name of the United States a civil action in any appropriate district court of the United States against such parties and for such relief as may be appropriate, and such court shall have and shall exercise jurisdiction of proceedings instituted pursuant to this section, provided that nothing herein shall empower any official or court of the United States to issue any order seeking to achieve a racial balance in any school by requiring the transportation of pupils or students from one school to another or one school district to another in order to achieve such racial balance, or otherwise enlarge the existing power of the court to insure compliance with constitutional standards. The Attorney General may implead as defendants such additional parties as are or become necessary to the grant of effective relief hereunder.

(b) The Attorney General may deem a person or persons unable to initiate and maintain appropriate legal proceedings within the meaning of subsection

(a) of this section when such person or persons are unable, either directly or through other interested persons or organizations, to bear the expense of the litigation or to obtain effective legal representation; or whenever he is satisfied that the institution of such litigation would jeopardize the personal safety, employment, or economic standing of such person or persons, their families, or their property.

(c) The term "parent" as used in this section includes any person standing in loco parentis. A "complaint" as used in this section is a writing or document within the meaning of section 1001, title 18, United States Code.

SEC. 408. In any action or proceeding under this title the United States shall be liable for costs the same as a private person.

SEC. 409. Nothing in this title shall affect adversely the right of any person to sue for or obtain relief in any court against discrimination in public education.

SEC. 410. Nothing in this title shall prohibit classification and assignment for reasons other than race, color, religion, or national origin.

Title V –– Commission on Civil Rights

SEC. 501. Section 102 of the Civil Rights Act of 1957 (42 U.S.C. 1975a; 71 Stat. 634) is amended to read as follows:

"Rules of Procedure of the Commission Hearings

"SEC. 102. (a) At least thirty days prior to the commencement of any hearing, the Commission shall cause to be published in the Federal Register notice of the date on which such hearing is to commence, the place at which it is to be held and the subject of the hearing. The Chairman, or one designated by him to act as Chairman at a hearing of the Commission, shall announce in an opening statement the subject of the hearing.

"(b) A copy of the Commission's rules shall be made available to any witness before the Commission, and a witness compelled to appear before the Commission or required to produce written or other matter shall be served with a copy of the Commission's rules at the time of service of the subpoena.

"(c) Any person compelled to appear in person before the Commission shall be accorded the right to be accompanied and advised by counsel, who shall have the right to subject his client to reasonable examination, and to make objections on the record and to argue briefly the basis for such objections. The Commission shall proceed with reasonable dispatch to conclude any hearing in which it is engaged. Due regard shall be had for the convenience and necessity of witnesses.

"(d) The Chairman or Acting Chairman may punish breaches of order and decorum by censure and exclusion from the hearings.

"(e) If the Commission determines that evidence or testimony at any hearing may tend to defame, degrade, or incriminate any person, it shall receive such evidence or testimony or summary of such evidence or testimony in executive session. The Commission shall afford any person defamed, degraded, or incriminated by such evidence or testimony an opportunity to appear and be heard in executive session, with a reasonable number of additional witnesses requested by him, before deciding to use such evidence or testimony. In the event the Commission determines to release or use such evidence or testimony in such manner as to reveal publicly the identity of the person defamed, degraded, or incriminated, such evidence or testimony, prior to such public release or use, shall be given at a public session, and the Commission shall afford such person an opportunity to appear as a voluntary witness or to file a sworn statement in his behalf and to submit brief and pertinent sworn statements of others. The Commission shall receive and dispose of requests from such person to subpoena additional witnesses.

"(f) Except as provided in sections 102 and 105 (f) of this Act, the Chairman shall receive and the Commission shall dispose of requests to subpoena additional witnesses.

"(g) No evidence or testimony or summary of evidence or testimony taken in executive session may be released or used in public sessions without the consent of the Commission. Whoever releases or uses in public without the consent of the Commission such evidence or testimony taken in executive session shall be fined not more than $1,000, or imprisoned for not more than one year.

"(h) In the discretion of the Commission, witnesses may submit brief and pertinent sworn statements in writing for inclusion in the record. The Commission shall determine the pertinency of testimony and evidence adduced at its hearings.

"(i) Every person who submits data or evidence shall be entitled to retain or, on payment of lawfully prescribed costs, procure a copy or transcript thereof, except that a witness in a hearing held in executive session may for good cause be limited to inspection of the official transcript of his testimony. Transcript copies of public sessions may be obtained by the public upon the payment of the cost thereof. An accurate transcript shall be made of the testimony of all witnesses at all hearings, either public or executive sessions, of the Commission or of any subcommittee thereof.

"(j) A witness attending any session of the Commission shall receive $6 for each day's attendance and for the time necessarily occupied in going to and returning from the same, and 10 cents per mile for going from and returning to his place of residence. Witnesses who attend at points so far removed from their respective residences as to prohibit return thereto from day to day shall be entitled to an additional allowance of $10 per day for expenses of subsistence including the time necessarily occupied in going to and returning from the place of attendance. Mileage payments shall be tendered to the witness upon service of a subpoena issued on behalf of the Commission or any subcommittee thereof.

"(k) The Commission shall not issue any subpoena for the attendance and testimony of witnesses or for the production of written or other matter which would require the presence of the party subpoenaed at a hearing to be held outside of the State wherein the witness is found or resides or is domiciled or transacts business, or has appointed an agent for receipt of service of process except that, in any event, the Commission may issue subpoenas for the attendance and testimony of witnesses and the production of written or other matter at a hearing held within fifty miles of the place where the witness is found or resides or is domiciled or transacts business or has appointed an agent for receipt of service of process.

"(l) The Commission shall separately state and currently publish in the Federal Register (1) descriptions of its central and field organization including the established places at which, and methods whereby, the public may secure information or make requests; (2) statements of the general course and method by which its functions are channeled and determined, and (3) rules adopted as authorized by law. No person shall in any manner be subject to or required to resort to rules, organization, or procedure not so published."

SEC. 502. Section 103(a) of the Civil Rights Act of 1957 (42 U.S.C. 1975b(a); 71 Stat. 634) is amended to read as follows:

"SEC. 103. (a) Each member of the Commission who is not otherwise in the service of the Government of the United States shall receive the sum of $75 per day for each day spent in the work of the Commission, shall be paid actual travel expenses, and per diem in lieu of subsistence expenses when away from his usual place of residence, in accordance with section 5 of the Administrative Expenses Act of 1946, as amended (5 U.S.C. 73b-2; 60 Stat. 808)."

SEC. 503. Section 103(b) of the Civil Rights Act of 1957 (42 U.S.C.

1975(b); 71 Stat. 634) is amended to read as follows:

"(b) Each member of the Commission who is otherwise in the service of the Government of the United States shall serve without compensation in addition to that received for such other service, but while engaged in the work of the Commission shall be paid actual travel expenses, and per diem in lieu of subsistence expenses when away from his usual place of residence, in accordance with the provisions of the Travel Expenses Act of 1949, as amended (5 U.S.C. 835 –– 42; 63 Stat. 166)."

SEC. 504. (a) Section 104(a) of the Civil Rights Act of 1957 (42 U.S.C. 1975c(a); 71 Stat. 635), as amended, is further amended to read as follows:

"Duties of the Commission

"SEC. 104. (a) The Commission shall ––

"(1) investigate allegations in writing under oath or affirmation that certain citizens of the United States are being deprived of their right to vote and have that vote counted by reason of their color, race, religion, or national origin; which writing, under oath or affirmation, shall set forth the facts upon which such belief or beliefs are based;

"(2) study and collect information concerning legal developments constituting a denial of equal protection of the laws under the Constitution because of race, color, religion or national origin or in the administration of justice;

"(3) appraise the laws and policies of the Federal Government with respect to denials of equal protection of the laws under the Constitution because of race, color, religion or national origin or in the administration of justice;

"(4) serve as a national clearinghouse for information in respect to denials of equal protection of the laws because of race, color, religion or national origin, including but not limited to the fields of voting, education, housing, employment, the use of public facilities, and transportation, or in the administration of justice;

"(5) investigate allegations, made in writing and under oath or affirmation, that citizens of the United States are unlawfully being accorded or denied the right to vote, or to have their votes properly counted, in any election of presidential electors, Members of the United States Senate, or of the House of Representatives, as a result of any patterns or practice of fraud or discrimination in the conduct of such election; and

"(6) Nothing in this or any other Act shall be construed as authorizing the Commission, its Advisory Committees, or any person under its supervision or control to inquire into or investigate any membership practices or internal operations of any fraternal organization, any college or university fraternity or sorority, any private club or any religious organization."

(b) Section 104(b) of the Civil Rights Act of 1957 (42 U.S.C. 1975c(b); 71 Stat. 635), as amended, is further amended by striking out the present subsection "(b)" and by substituting therefor:

"(b) The Commission shall submit interim reports to the President and to the Congress at such times as the Commission, the Congress or the President shall deem desirable, and shall submit to the President and to the Congress a final report of its activities, findings, and recommendations not later than January 31, 1968."

SEC. 505. Section 105(a) of the Civil Rights Act of 1957 (42 U.S.C. 1975d(a); 71 Stat. 636) is amended by striking out in the last sentence thereof "$50 per diem" and inserting in lieu thereof "$75 per diem."

SEC. 506. Section 105(f) and section 105(g) of the Civil Rights Act of 1957 (42 U.S.C. 1975d (f) and (g); 71 Stat. 636) are amended to read as follows:

"(f) The Commission, or on the authorization of the Commission any subcommittee of two or more members, at least one of whom shall be of each major political party, may, for the purpose of carrying out the provisions of this Act, hold such hearings and act at such times and places as the Commission or such authorized subcommittee may deem advisable. Subpoenas for the attendance and testimony of witnesses or the production of written or other matter may be issued in accordance with the rules of the Commission as contained in section 102 (j) and (k) of this Act, over the signature of the Chairman of the Commission or of such subcommittee, and may be served by any person designated by such Chairman. The holding of hearings by the Commission, or the appointment of a subcommittee to hold hearings pursuant to this subparagraph, must be approved by a majority of the Commission, or by a majority of the members present at a meeting at which at least a quorum of four members is present.

"(g) In case of contumacy or refusal to obey a subpoena, any district court of the United States or the United States court of any territory or possession, or the District Court of the United States for the District of Columbia, within the jurisdiction of which the inquiry is carried on or within the jurisdiction of which said person guilty of contumacy or refusal to obey is found or resides or is domiciled or transacts business, or has appointed an agent for receipt of service of process, upon application by the Attorney General of the United States shall have jurisdiction to issue to such person an order requiring such person to appear before the Commission or a subcommittee thereof, there to produce pertinent, relevant and non-privileged evidence if so ordered, or there to give testimony touching the matter under investigation; and any failure to obey such order of the court may be punished by said court as a contempt thereof."

SEC. 507. Section 105 of the Civil Rights Act of 1957 (42 U.S.C.1975d; 71 Stat. 636), as amended by section 401 of the Civil Rights Act of 1960 (42 U.S.C. 1975d(h); 74 Stat. 89), is further amended by adding a new subsection at the end to read as follows:

"(i) The Commission shall have the power to make such rules and regulations as are necessary to carry out the purposes of this Act."

Title VI –– Nondiscrimination in Federally Assisted Programs

SEC. 601. No person in the United States shall, on the ground of race, color, or national origin, be excluded from participation in, be denied the benefits of, or be subjected to discrimination under any program or activity receiving Federal financial assistance.

SEC. 602. Each Federal department and agency which is empowered to extend Federal financial assistance to any program or activity, by way of grant, loan, or contract other than a contract of insurance or guaranty, is authorized and directed to effectuate the provisions of section 601 with respect to such program or activity by issuing rules, regulations, or orders of general applicability which shall be consistent with achievement of the objectives of the statute authorizing the financial assistance in connection with which the action is taken. No such rule, regulation, or order shall become effective unless and until approved by the President. Compliance with any requirement adopted pursuant to this section may be effected (1) by the termination of or refusal to grant or to continue assistance under such program or activity to any recipient as to whom there has been an express finding on the record, after opportunity for hearing, of a failure to comply with such requirement, but such termination or refusal shall be limited to the particular political entity, or part thereof, or other recipient as to whom such a finding has been made and, shall be limited in its effect to the particular program, or part thereof, in which such non-compliance has been so found, or (2) by any other means authorized by law: Provided, however, That no such action shall be taken until the department or agency concerned has advised the appropriate person or persons of the failure to comply with the requirement and has determined that compliance cannot be secured by voluntary means. In the case of any action terminating, or refusing to grant or continue, assistance because of failure to comply with a requirement imposed pursuant to this section, the head of the federal department or agency shall file with the committees of the House and Senate having legislative jurisdiction over the program or activity involved a full written report of the circumstances and the grounds for such action. No such action shall become effective until thirty days have elapsed after the filing of such report.

SEC. 603. Any department or agency action taken pursuant to section 602 shall be subject to such judicial review as may otherwise be provided by law for similar action taken by such department or agency on other grounds. In the case of action, not otherwise subject to judicial review, terminating or refusing to grant or to continue financial assistance upon a finding of failure to comply with any requirement imposed pursuant to section 602, any person aggrieved (including any State or political subdivision thereof and any agency of either) may obtain judicial review of such action in accordance with section 10 of the Administrative Procedure Act, and such action shall not be deemed committed to unreviewable agency discretion within the meaning of that section.

SEC. 604. Nothing contained in this title shall be construed to authorize action under this title by any department or agency with respect to any employment practice of any employer, employment agency, or labor organization except where a primary objective of the Federal financial assistance is to provide employment.

SEC. 605. Nothing in this title shall add to or detract from any existing authority with respect to any program or activity under which Federal financial assistance is extended by way of a contract of insurance or guaranty.

TITLE VII –– EQUAL EMPLOYMENT OPPORTUNITY

Definitions

SEC. 701. For the purposes of this title ––
(a) The term "person" includes one or more individuals, labor unions, partnerships, associations, corporations, legal representatives, mutual companies, joint-stock companies, trusts, unincorporated organizations, trustees, trustees in bankruptcy, or receivers.
(b) The term "employer" means a person engaged in an industry affecting commerce who

has twenty-five or more employees for each working day in each of twenty or more calendar weeks in the current or preceding calendar year, and any agent of such a person, but such term does not include (1) the United States, a corporation wholly owned by the Government of the United States, an Indian tribe, or a State or political subdivision thereof, (2) a bona fide private membership club (other than a labor organization) which is exempt from taxation under section 501(c) of the Internal Revenue Code of 1954: Provided, That during the first year after the effective date prescribed in subsection (a) of section 716, persons having fewer than one hundred employees (and their agents) shall not be considered employers, and, during the second year after such date, persons having fewer than seventy-five employees (and their agents) shall not be considered employers, and, during the third year after such date, persons having fewer than fifty employees (and their agents) shall not be considered employers: Provided further, That it shall be the policy of the United States to insure equal employment opportunities for Federal employees without discrimination because of race, color, religion, sex or national origin and the President shall utilize his existing authority to effectuate this policy.

(c) The term "employment agency" means any person regularly undertaking with or without compensation to procure employees for an employer or to procure for employees opportunities to work for an employer and includes an agent of such a person; but shall not include an agency of the United States, or an agency of a State or political subdivision of a State, except that such term shall include the United States Employment Service and the system of State and local employment services receiving Federal assistance.

(d) The term "labor organization" means a labor organization engaged in an industry affecting commerce, and any agent of such an organization, and includes any organization of any kind, any agency, or employee representation committee, group, association, or plan so engaged in which employees participate and which exists for the purpose, in whole or in part, of dealing with employers concerning grievances, labor disputes, wages, rates of pay, hours, or other terms or conditions of employment, and any conference, general committee, joint or system board, or joint council so engaged which is subordinate to a national or international labor organization.

(c) A labor organization shall be deemed to be engaged in an industry affecting commerce if (1) it maintains or operates a hiring hall or hiring office which procures employees for an employer or procures for employees opportunities to work for an employer, or (2) the number of its members (or, where it is a labor organization composed of other labor organizations or their representatives, if the aggregate number of the members of such other labor organization) is (A) one hundred or more during the first year after the effective date prescribed in subsection (a) of section 716, (B) seventy-five or more during the second year after such date or fifty or more during the third year, or (C) twenty-five or more thereafter, and such labor organization ––

(1) is the certified representative of employees under the provisions of the National Labor Relations Act, as amended, or the Railway Labor Act, as amended;

(2) although not certified, is a national or international labor organization or a local labor organization recognized or acting as the representative of employees of an employer or employers engaged in an industry affecting commerce; or

(3) has chartered a local labor organization or subsidiary body which is representing or actively seeking to represent employees of employers within the meaning of paragraph (1) or (2); or

(4) has been chartered by a labor organization representing or actively seeking to represent employees within the meaning of paragraph (1) or (2) as the local or subordinate body through which such employees may enjoy membership or become affiliated with such labor organization; or

(5) is a conference, general committee, joint or system board, or joint council subordinate to a national or international labor organization, which includes a labor organization engaged in an industry affecting commerce within the meaning of any of the preceding paragraphs of this subsection.

(f) The term "employee" means an individual employed by an employer.

(g) The term "commerce" means trade, traffic, commerce, transportation, transmission, or communication among the several States; or between a State and any place outside thereof; or within the District of Columbia, or a possession of the United States; or between points in the same State but through a point outside thereof.

(h) The term "industry affecting commerce" means any activity, business, or industry in commerce or in which a labor dispute would hinder or obstruct commerce or the free flow of commerce and includes any activity or industry "affecting commerce" within the meaning of the Labor-Management Reporting and Disclosure Act of 1959.

(i) The term "State" includes a State of the United States, the District of Columbia, Puerto Rico, the Virgin Islands, American Samoa, Guam, Wake Island, The Canal Zone, and Outer Continental Shelf Lands defined in the Outer Continental Shelf Lands Act.

Exemption

SEC. 702. This title shall not apply to an employer with respect to the employment of aliens outside any State, or to a religious corporation, association, or society with respect to the employment of individuals of a particular religion to perform work connected with the carrying on by such corporation, association, or society of its religious activities or to an educational institution with respect to the employment of individuals to perform work connected with the educational activities of such institution.

Discrimination Because of Race, Color, Religion, Sex, or National Origin

SEC. 703. (a) It shall be an unlawful employment practice for an employer ––

(1) to fail or refuse to hire or to discharge any individual, or otherwise to discriminate against any individual with respect to his compensation, terms, conditions, or privileges of employment, because of such individual's race, color, religion, sex, or national origin; or

(2) to limit, segregate, or classify his employees in any way which would deprive or tend to deprive any individual of employment opportunities or otherwise adversely affect his status as an employee, because of such individual's race, color, religion, sex, or national origin.

(b) It shall be an unlawful employment practice for an employment agency to fail or refuse to refer for employment, or otherwise to discriminate against, any individual because of his race, color, religion, sex, or national origin, or to classify or refer for employment any individual on the basis of his race, color, religion, sex, or national origin.

(c) It shall be an unlawful employment practice for a labor organization ––

(l) to exclude or to expel from its membership, or otherwise to discriminate against, any individual because of his race, color, religion, sex, or national origin;

(2) to limit, segregate, or classify its membership, or to classify or fail or refuse to refer for employment any individual, in any way which would deprive or tend to deprive any individual of employment opportunities, or would limit such employment opportunities or otherwise adversely affect his status as an employee or as an applicant for employment, because of such individual's race, color, religion, sex, or national origin; or

(3) to cause or attempt to cause an employer to discriminate against an individual in violation of this section.

(d) It shall be an unlawful employment practice for any employer, labor organization, or joint labor-management committee controlling apprenticeship or other training or retraining, including on-the-job training programs to discriminate against any individual because of his race, color, religion, sex, or national origin in admission to, or employment in, any program established to provide apprenticeship or other training.

(c) Notwithstanding any other provision of this title, (1) it shall not be an unlawful employment practice for an employer to hire and employ employees, for an employment agency to classify, or refer for employment any individual, for a labor organization to classify its membership or to classify or refer for employment any individual, or for an employer, labor organization, or joint labor-management committee controlling apprenticeship or other training or retraining programs to admit or employ any individual in any such program, on the basis of his religion, sex, or national origin in those certain instances where religion, sex, or national origin is a bona fide occupational qualification reasonably necessary to the normal operation of that particular business or enterprise, and (2) it shall not be an unlawful employment practice for a school, college, university, or other educational institution or institution of learning to hire and employ employees of a particular religion if such school, college, university, or other educational institution or institution of learning is, in whole or in substantial part, owned, supported, controlled, or managed by a particular religion or by a particular religious corporation, association, or society, or if the curriculum of such school, college, university, or other educational institution or institution of learning is directed toward the propagation of a particular religion.

(f) As used in this title, the phrase "unlawful employment practice" shall not be deemed to include any action or measure taken by an employer, labor organization, joint labor-management committee, or employment agency with respect to an individual who is a member of the Communist Party of the United States or of any other organization required to register as a Communist-action or Communist-front organization by final order of the Subversive Activities Control Board pursuant to the Subversive Activities Control Act of 1950.

(g) Notwithstanding any other provision of this title, it shall not be an unlawful employment practice for an employer to fail or refuse to hire and employ any individual for any position, for an employer to discharge any individual from any position, or for an employment agency to fail or refuse to refer any individual for employment in any position, or for a labor organization to fail or refuse to refer any individual for employment in any position, if —

(1) the occupancy of such position, or access to the premises in or upon which any part of the duties of such position is performed or is to be performed, is subject to any requirement imposed in the interest of the national security of the United States under any security program in effect pursuant to or administered under any statute of the United States or any Executive order of the President; and

(2) such individual has not fulfilled or has ceased to fulfill that requirement.

(h) Notwithstanding any other provision of this title, it shall not be an unlawful employment practice for an employer to apply different standards of compensation, or different terms, conditions, or privileges of employment pursuant to a bona fide seniority or merit system, or a system which measures earnings by quantity or quality of production or to employees who work in different locations, provided that such differences are not the result of an intention to discriminate because of race, color, religion, sex, or national origin, nor shall it be an unlawful employment practice for an employer to give and to act upon the results of any professionally developed ability test provided that such test, its administration or action upon the results is not designed, intended or used to discriminate because of race, color, religion, sex or national origin. It shall not be an unlawful employment practice under this title for any employer to differentiate upon the basis of sex in determining the amount of the wages or compensation paid or to be paid to employees of such employer if such differentiation is authorized by the provisions of section 6(d) of the Fair Labor Standards Act of 1938, as amended (29 U.S.C. 206(d)).

(i) Nothing contained in this title shall apply to any business or enterprise on or near an Indian reservation with respect to any publicly announced employment practice of such business or enterprise under which a preferential treatment is given to any individual because he is an Indian living on or near a reservation.

(j) Nothing contained in this title shall be interpreted to require any employer, employment agency, labor organization, or joint labor-management committee subject to this title to grant preferential treatment to any individual or to any group because of the race, color, religion, sex, or national origin of such individual or group on account of an imbalance which may exist with respect to the total number or percentage of persons of any race, color, religion, sex, or national origin employed by any employer, referred or classified for employment by any employment agency or labor organization, admitted to membership or classified by any labor organization, or admitted to, or employed in, any apprenticeship or other training program, in comparison with the total number or percentage of persons of such race, color, religion, sex, or national origin in any community, State, section, or other area, or in the available work force in any community, State, section, or other area.

Other Unlawful Employment Practices

SEC. 704. (a) It shall be an unlawful employment practice for an employer to discriminate against any of his employees or applicants for employment, for an employment agency to discriminate against any individual, or for a labor organization to discriminate against any member thereof or applicant for membership, because he has opposed, any practice made an unlawful employment practice by this title, or because he has made a charge, testified, assisted, or participated in any manner in an investigation, proceeding, or hearing under this title.

(b) It shall be an unlawful employment practice for an employer, labor organization, or employment agency to print or publish or cause to be printed or published any notice or advertisement relating to employment by such an employer or membership in or any classification or referral for employment by such a labor organization, or relating to any classification or referral for employment by such an employment agency, indicating any preference, limitation, specification, or discrimination, based on race, color, religion, sex, or national origin, except that such a notice or advertisement may indicate a preference, limitation, specification, or discrimination based on religion, sex, or national origin when religion, sex, or national origin is a bona fide occupational qualification for employment.

Equal Employment Opportunity Commission

SEC. 705. (a) There is hereby created a Commission to be known as the Equal Employment Opportunity Commission, which shall be composed of five members, not more than three of whom shall be members of the same political party, who shall be appointed by the President by and with the advice and consent of the Senate. One of the original members shall be appointed for a term of one year, one for a term of two years, one for a term of three years, one for a term of four years, and one for a term of five years, beginning from the date of enactment of this title, but their successors shall be appointed for terms of five years each, except that any individual chosen to fill a vacancy shall be appointed only for the unexpired term of the member whom he shall succeed. The President shall designate one member to serve as Chairman of the Commission, and one member to serve as Vice Chairman. The Chairman shall be responsible on behalf of the Commission for the administrative operations of the Commission, and shall appoint, in accordance with the civil service laws, such officers, agents, attorneys, and employees as it deems necessary to assist it in the performance of its functions and to fix their compensation in accordance with the Classification Act of 1949, as amended. The Vice Chairman shall act as Chairman in the absence or disability of the Chairman or in the event of a vacancy in that office.

(b) A vacancy in the Commission shall not impair the right of the remaining members to exercise all the powers of the Commission and three members thereof shall constitute a quorum.

(c) The Commission shall have an official seal which shall be judicially noticed.

(d) The Commission shall at the close of each fiscal year report to the Congress and to the President concerning the action it has taken; the names, salaries, and duties of all individuals in its employ and the moneys it has disbursed; and shall make such further reports on the cause of and means of eliminating discrimination and such recommendations for further legislation as may appear desirable.

(e) The Federal Executive Pay Act of 1956, as amended (5 U.S.C. 2201–2209), is further amended —

(1) by adding to section 105 thereof (5 U.S.C. 2204) the following clause:

"(32) Chairman, Equal Employment Opportunity Commission"; and

(2) by adding to clause (45) of section 106(a) thereof (5 U.S.C. 2205(a)) the following: "Equal Employment Opportunity Commission (4)."

(f) The principal office of the Commission shall be in or near the District of Columbia, but it may meet or exercise any or all its powers at any other place. The Commission may establish such regional or State offices as it deems necessary to accomplish the purpose of this title.

(g) The Commission shall have power —

(l) to cooperate with and, with their consent, utilize regional, State, local, and other agencies, both public and private, and individuals;

(2) to pay to witnesses whose depositions are taken or who are summoned before the Commission or any of its agents the same witness and mileage fees as are paid to witnesses in the courts of the United States;

(3) to furnish to persons subject to this title such technical assistance as they may request to further their compliance with this title or an order issued thereunder;

(4) upon the request of (i) any employer, whose employees or some of them, or (ii) any labor organization, whose members or some of them, refuse or threaten to refuse to cooperate in effectuating the provisions of this title, to assist in such effectuation by conciliation or such other remedial action as is provided by this title;

(5) to make such technical studies as are appropriate to effectuate the purposes and policies of this title and to make the results of such studies available to the public;

(6) to refer matters to the Attorney General with recommendations for intervention in a civil action brought by an aggrieved party under section 706, or for the institution of a civil action by the Attorney General under section 707, and to advise, consult, and assist the Attorney General on such matters.

(h) Attorneys appointed under this section may, at the direction of the Commission, appear for and represent the Commission in any case in court.

(i) The Commission shall, in any of its educational or promotional activities, cooperate with other departments and agencies in the performance of such educational and promotional activities.

(j) All officers, agents, attorneys, and employees of the Commission shall be subject to the provisions of section 9 of the Act of August 2, 1939, as amended (the Hatch Act), notwithstanding any exemption contained in such section.

Prevention of Unlawful Employment Practices

SEC. 706. (a) Whenever it is charged in writing under oath by a person claiming to be aggrieved, or a written charge has been filed by a member of the Commission where he has reasonable cause to believe a violation of this title has occurred (and such charge sets forth the facts upon which it is based) that an employer, employment agency, or labor organization has engaged in an unlawful employment practice, the Commission shall furnish such employer, employment agency, or labor organization (hereinafter referred to as the "respondent") with a copy of such charge and shall make an investigation of such charge, provided that such charge shall not be made public by the Commission. If the Commission shall determine, after such investigation, that there is reasonable cause to believe that the charge is true, the Commission shall endeavor to eliminate any such alleged unlawful employment practice by informal methods of conference, conciliation, and persuasion. Nothing said or done during and as a part of such endeavors may be made public by the Commission without the written consent of the parties, or used as evidence in a subsequent proceeding. Any officer or employee of the Commission, who shall make public in any manner whatever any information in violation of this subsection shall be deemed guilty of a misdemeanor and upon conviction thereof shall be fined not more than $1,000 or imprisoned not more than one year.

(b) In the case of an alleged unlawful employment practice occurring in a State, or political subdivision of a State, which has a State or local law prohibiting the unlawful employment practice alleged and establishing or authorizing a State or local authority to grant or seek relief from such practice or to institute criminal proceedings with respect thereto upon receiving notice thereof, no charge may be filed under subsection (a) by the person aggrieved before the expiration of sixty days after proceedings have been commenced under the State or local law, unless such proceedings have been earlier terminated, provided that such sixty-day period shall be extended to one hundred and twenty days during the first year after the effective date of such State or local law. If any requirement for the commencement of such proceedings is imposed by a State or local authority other than a requirement of the filing of a written and signed statement of the facts upon which the proceeding is based, the proceeding shall be deemed to have been commenced for the purposes of this subsection at the time such statement is sent by registered mail to the appropriate State or local authority.

(c) In the case of any charge filed by a member of the Commission alleging an unlawful employment practice occurring in a State or political subdivision of a State, which has a State or local law prohibiting the practice alleged and establishing or authorizing a State or local authority to grant or seek relief from such practice or to institute criminal proceedings with respect thereto upon receiving notice thereof, the Commission shall, before taking any action with respect to such charge, notify the appropriate State or local officials and, upon request, afford them a reasonable time, but not less than sixty days (provided that such sixty-day period shall be extended to one hundred and twenty days during the first year after the effective day of such State or local law), unless a shorter period is requested, to act under such State or local law to remedy the practice alleged.

(d) A charge under subsection (a) shall be filed within ninety days after the alleged unlawful employment practice occurred, except that in the case of an unlawful employment practice with respect to which the person aggrieved has followed the procedure set out in subsection (b), such charge shall be filed by the person aggrieved within two hundred and ten days after the alleged unlawful employment practice occurred, or within thirty days after receiving notice that the State or local agency has terminated the proceedings under the State or local law, whichever is earlier, and a copy of such charge shall be filed by the Commission with the State or local agency.

(e) If within thirty days after a charge is filed with the Commission or within thirty days after expiration of any period of reference under subsection (c) (except that in either case such period may be extended to not more than sixty days upon a determination by the Commission that further efforts to secure voluntary compliance are warranted), the Commission has been unable to obtain voluntary compliance with this title, the Commission shall so notify the person aggrieved and a civil action may, within thirty days thereafter, be brought against the respondent named in the charge (1) by the person claiming to be aggrieved, or (2) if such charge was filed by a member of the Commission, by any person whom the charge alleges was aggrieved by the alleged unlawful employment practice. Upon application by the complainant and in such circumstances as the court may deem just, the court may appoint an attorney for such complainant and may authorize the commencement of the action without the payment of fees, costs, or security. Upon timely application, the court may, in its discretion, permit the Attorney General to intervene in such civil action if he certifies that the case is of general public importance. Upon request, the court may, in its discretion, stay further proceedings for not more than sixty days pending the termination of State or local proceedings described in subsection (b) or the efforts of the Commission to obtain voluntary compliance.

(f) Each United States district court and each United States court of a place subject to the jurisdiction of the United States shall have jurisdiction of actions brought under this title. Such an action may be brought in any judicial district in the State in which the unlawful employment practice is alleged to have been committed, in the judicial district in which the employment records relevant to such practice are maintained and administered, or in the judicial district in which the plaintiff would have worked but for the alleged unlawful employment practice, but if the respondent is not found within any such district, such an action may be brought within the judicial district in which the respondent has his principal office. For purposes of sections 1404 and 1406 of title 28 of the United States Code, the judicial district in which the respondent has his principal office shall in all cases be considered a district in which the action might have been brought.

(g) If the court finds that the respondent has intentionally engaged in or is intentionally engaging in an unlawful employment practice charged in the complaint, the court may enjoin the respondent from engaging in such unlawful employment practice, and order such affirmative action as may be appropriate, which may include reinstatement or hiring of employees, with or without back pay (payable by the employer, employment agency, or labor organization, as the case may be, responsible for the unlawful employment practice). Interim earnings or amounts earnable with reasonable diligence by the person or persons discriminated against shall operate to reduce the back pay otherwise allowable. No order of the court shall require the admission or reinstatement of an individual as a member of a union or the hiring, reinstatement, or promotion of an individual as an employee, or the payment to him of any back pay, if such individual was refused admission, suspended, or expelled or was refused employment or advancement or was suspended or discharged for any reason other than discrimination on account of race, color, religion, sex or national origin or in violation of section 704(a).

(h) The provisions of the Act entitled "An Act to amend the Judicial Code and to define and limit the jurisdiction of courts sitting in equity, and for other purposes," approved March 23, 1932 (29 U.S.C. 101–115), shall not apply with respect to civil actions brought under this section.

(i) In any case in which an employer, employment agency, or labor organization fails to comply with an order of a court issued in a civil action brought under subsection (e), the Commission may commence proceedings to compel compliance with such order.

(j) Any civil action brought under subsection (e) and any proceedings brought under subsection (i) shall be subject to appeal as provided in sections 1291 and 1292, title 28, United States Code.

(k) In any action or proceeding under this title the court, in its discretion, may allow the prevailing party, other than the Commission or the United States, a reasonable attorney's fee as part of the costs, and the Commission and the United States shall be liable for costs the same as a private person.

SEC. 707. (a) Whenever the Attorney General has reasonable cause to believe that any person or group of persons is engaged in a pattern or practice of resistance to the full enjoyment of any of the rights secured by this title, and that the pattern or practice is of such a nature and is intended to deny the full exercise of the rights herein described, the Attorney General may bring a civil action in the appropriate district court of the United States by filing with it a complaint (1) signed by him (or in his absence the Acting Attorney General), (2) setting forth facts pertaining to such pattern or practice, and (3) requesting such relief, including an application for a permanent or temporary injunction, restraining order or other order against the person or persons responsible for such pattern or practice, as he deems necessary to insure the full enjoyment of the rights herein described.

(b) The district courts of the United States shall have and shall exercise jurisdiction of proceedings instituted pursuant to this section, and in any such proceeding the Attorney General may file with the clerk of such court a request that a court of three judges be convened to hear and determine the case. Such request by the Attorney General shall be accompanied by a certificate that, in his opinion, the case is of general public importance. A copy of the certificate and request for a three-judge court shall be immediately furnished by such clerk to the chief judge of the circuit (or in his absence, the presiding circuit judge of the circuit) in which the case is pending. Upon receipt of such request it shall be the duty of the chief judge of the circuit or the presiding circuit judge, as the case may be, to designate immediately three judges in such circuit, of whom at least one shall be a circuit judge and another of whom shall be a district judge of the court in which the proceeding was instituted, to hear and determine such case, and it shall be the duty of the judges so designated to assign the case for hearing at the earliest practicable date, to participate in the hearing and determination thereof, and to cause the case to be in every way expedited. An appeal from the final judgment of such court will lie to the Supreme Court.

In the event the Attorney General fails to file such a request in any such proceeding, it shall be the duty of the chief judge of the district (or in his absence, the acting chief judge) in which the case is pending immediately to designate a judge in such district to hear and determine the case. In the event that no judge in the district is available to hear and determine the case, the chief judge of the district, or the acting chief judge, as the case may be, shall certify this fact to the chief judge of the circuit (or in his absence, the acting chief judge) who shall then designate a district or circuit judge of the circuit to hear and determine the case.

It shall be the duty of the judge designated pursuant to this section to assign the case for hearing at the earliest practicable date and to cause the case to be in every way expedited.

Effect on State Laws

SEC. 708. Nothing in this title shall be deemed to exempt or relieve any person from any liability, duty, penalty, or punishment provided by any present or future law of any State or political subdivision of a State, other than any such law which purports to require or permit the doing of any act which would be an unlawful employment practice under this title.

Investigation, Inspections, Records, State Agencies

SEC. 709. (a) In connection with any investigation of a charge filed under section 706, the Commission or its designated representative shall at all reasonable times have access to, for the purposes of examination, and the right to copy any evidence of any person being investigated or proceeded against that relates to unlawful employment practices covered by this title and is relevant to the charge under investigation.

(b) The Commission may cooperate with State and local agencies charged with the administration of State fair employment practices laws and, with the consent of such agencies, may for the purpose of carrying out its functions and duties under this title and within the limitation of funds appropriated specifically for such purpose, utilize the services of such agencies and their employees and, notwithstanding any other provision of law, may reimburse such agencies and their employees for services rendered to assist the Commission in carrying out this title. In furtherance of such cooperative efforts, the Commission may enter into written agreements with such State or local agencies and such agreements may include provisions under which the Commission shall refrain from processing a charge in any cases or class of cases specified in such agreements and under which no person may bring a civil action under section 706 in any cases or class of cases so specified, or under which the Commission shall relieve any person or class of persons in such State or locality from requirements imposed under this section. The Commission shall rescind any such agreement whenever it determines that the agreement no longer serves the interest of effective enforcement of this title.

(c) Except as provided in subsection (d), every employer, employment agency, and labor organization subject to this title shall (1) make and keep such records relevant to the determinations of whether unlawful employment practices have been or are being committed, (2) preserve such records for such periods, and (3) make such reports therefrom, as the Commission shall prescribe by regulation or order, after public hearing, as reasonable, necessary, or appropriate for the enforcement of this title or the regulations or orders thereunder. The Commission shall, by regulation, require each employer, labor organization, and joint labor-management committee subject to this title which controls an apprenticeship or other training program to maintain such records as are reasonably necessary to carry out the purpose of this title, including, but not limited to, a list of applicants who wish to participate in such program, including the chronological order in which such applications were received, and shall furnish to the Commission, upon request, a detailed description of the manner in which persons are selected to participate in the apprenticeship or other training program. Any employer, employment agency, labor organization, or joint labor-management committee which believes that the application to it of any regulation or order issued under this section would result in undue hardship may (1) apply to the Commission for an exemption from the application of such regulation or order, or (2) bring a civil action in the United States district court for the district where such records are kept. If the Commission or the court, as the case may be, finds that the application of the regulation or order to the employer, employment agency, or labor organization in question would impose an undue hardship, the Commission or the court, as the case may be, may grant appropriate relief.

(d) The provisions of subsection (c) shall not apply to any employer, employment agency, labor organization, or joint labor-management committee with respect to matters occurring in any State or political subdivision thereof which has a fair employment practice law during any period in which such employer, employment agency, labor organization, or joint labor-management committee is subject to such law, except that the Commission may require such notations on records which such employer, employment agency, labor organization, or joint labor-management committee keeps or is required to keep as are necessary because of differences in coverage or methods of enforcement between the State or local law and the provisions of this title. Where an employer is required by Executive Order 10925, issued March 6, 1961, or by any other Executive order prescribing fair employment practices for Government contractors and subcontractors, or by rules or regulations issued thereunder, to file reports relating to his employment practices with any Federal agency or committee, and he is substantially in compliance with such requirements, the Commission shall not require him to file additional reports pursuant to subsection (c) of this section.

(e) It shall be unlawful for any officer or employee of the Commission to make public in any manner whatever any information obtained by the Commission pursuant to its authority under this section prior to the institution of any proceeding under this title involving such information. Any officer or employee of the Commission who shall make public in any manner whatever any information in violation of this subsection shall be guilty of a misdemeanor and, upon conviction thereof, shall be fined not more than $1,000, or imprisoned not more than one year.

Investigatory Powers

SEC. 710. (a) For the purposes of any investigation of a charge filed under the authority contained in section 706, the Commission shall have authority to examine witnesses under oath and to require the production of documentary evidence relevant or material to the charge under investigation.

(b) If the respondent named in a charge filed under section 706 fails or refuses to comply with a demand of the Commission for permission to examine or to copy evidence in conformity with the provisions of section 709(a), or if any person required to comply with the provisions of section 709 (c) or (d) fails or refuses to do so, or if any person fails or refuses to comply with a demand by the Commission to give testimony under oath, the United States district court for the district in which such person is found, resides, or transacts business, shall, upon application of the Commission, have jurisdiction to issue to such person an order requiring him to comply with the provisions of section 709 (c) or (d) or to comply with the demand of the Commission, but the attendance of a witness may not be required outside the State where he is found, resides, or transacts business and the production of evidence may not be required outside the State where such evidence is kept.

(c) Within twenty days after the service upon any person charged under section 706 of a demand by the Commission for the production of documentary evidence or for permission to examine or to copy evidence in conformity with the provisions of section 709(a), such person may file in the district court of the United States for the judicial district in which he resides, is found, or transacts business, and serve upon the Commission a petition for an order of such court modifying or setting aside such demand. The time allowed for compliance with the demand in whole or in part as deemed proper and ordered by the court shall not run during the pendency of such petition in the court. Such petition shall specify each ground upon which the petitioner relies in seeking such relief, and may be based upon any failure of such demand to comply with the provisions of this title or with the limitations generally applicable to compulsory process or upon any constitutional or other legal right or privilege of such person. No objection which is not raised by such a petition may be urged in the defense to a proceeding initiated by the Commission under subsection (b) for enforcement of such a demand unless such proceeding is commenced by the Commission prior to the expiration of the twenty-day period, or unless the court determines that the defendant could not reasonably have been aware of the availability of such ground of objection.

(d) In any proceeding brought by the Commission under subsection (b), except as provided in subsection (c) of this section, the defendant may petition the court for an order modifying or setting aside the demand of the Commission.

SEC. 711. (a) Every employer, employment agency, and labor organization, as the case may be, shall post and keep posted in conspicuous places upon its premises where notices to employees, applicants for employment, and members are customarily posted a notice to be prepared or approved by the Commission setting forth excerpts from, or summaries of, the pertinent provisions of this title and information pertinent to the filing of a complaint.

(b) A willful violation of this section shall be punishable by a fine of not more than $100 for each separate offense.

Veterans' Preference

SEC. 712. Nothing contained in this title shall be construed to repeal or modify any Federal, State, territorial, or local law creating special rights or preference for veterans.

Rules and Regulations

SEC. 713. (a) The Commission shall have authority from time to time to issue, amend, or rescind suitable procedural regulations to carry out the provisions of this title. Regulations issued under this section shall be in conformity with the standards and limitations of the Administrative Procedure Act.

(b) In any action or proceeding based on any alleged unlawful employment practice, no person shall be subject to any liability or punishment for or on account of (1) the commission by such person of an unlawful employment practice if he pleads and proves that the act or omission complained of was in good faith, in conformity with, and in reliance on any written interpretation or opinion of the Commission, or (2) the failure of such person to publish and file any information required by any provision of this title if he pleads and proves that he failed to publish and file such information in good faith, in conformity with the instructions of the Commission issued under this title regarding the filing of such information. Such a defense, if established, shall be a bar to the action or proceeding, notwithstanding that (A) after such act or omission, such interpretation or opinion is modified or rescinded or is determined by judicial authority to be invalid or of no legal effect, or (B) after publishing or filing the description and annual reports, such publication or filing is determined by judicial authority not to be in conformity with the requirements of this title.

Forcibly Resisting the Commission or its Representatives

SEC. 714. The provisions of section 111, title 18, United States Code, shall apply to officers, agents, and employees of the Commission in the performance of their official duties.

Special Study by Secretary of Labor

SEC. 715. The Secretary of Labor shall make a full and complete study of the factors which might tend to result in discrimination in employment because of age and of the consequences of such discrimination on the economy and individuals affected. The Secretary of Labor shall make a report to the Congress not later than June 30, 1965, containing the results of such study and shall include in such report such recommendations for legislation to prevent arbitrary discrimination in employment because of age as he determines advisable.

Effective Date

SEC. 716. (a) This title shall become effective one year after the date of its enactment.

(b) Notwithstanding subsection (a), sections of this title other than sections 703, 704, 706, and 707 shall become effective immediately.

(c) The President shall, as soon as feasible after the enactment of this title, convene one or more conferences for the purpose of enabling the leaders of groups whose members will be affected by this title to become familiar with the rights afforded and obligations imposed by its provisions, and for the purpose of making plans which will result in the fair and effective administration of this title when all of its provisions become effective. The President shall invite the participation in such conference or conferences of (1) the members of the President's Committee on Equal Employment Opportunity, (2) the members of the Commission on Civil Rights, (3) representatives of State and local agencies engaged in furthering equal employment opportunity, (4) representatives of private agencies engaged in furthering equal employment opportunity, and (5) representatives of employers, labor organizations, and employment agencies who will be subject to this title.

Title VIII –– Registration and Voting Statistics

SEC. 801. The Secretary of Commerce shall promptly conduct a survey to compile registration and voting statistics in such geographic areas as may be recommended by the Commission on Civil Rights. Such a survey and compilation shall, to the extent recommended by the Commission on Civil Rights, only include a count of persons of voting age by race, color, and national origin, and determination of the extent to which such persons are registered to vote, and have voted in any statewide primary or general election in which the Members of the United States House of Representatives are nominated or elected, since January 1, 1960. Such information shall also be collected and compiled in connection with the Nineteenth Decennial Census, and at such other times as the Congress may prescribe. The provisions of section 9 and chapter 7 of title 13, United States Code, shall apply to any survey, collection, or compilation of registration and voting statistics carried out under this title: Provided, however, That no person shall be compelled to disclose his race, color, national origin, or questioned about his political party affiliation, how he voted, or the reasons therefore, nor shall any penalty be imposed for his failure or refusal to make such disclosure. Every person interrogated orally, by written survey or questionnaire or by any other means with respect to such information shall be fully advised with respect to his right to fail or refuse to furnish such information.

Title IX –– Intervention and Procedure After Removal in Civil Rights Cases

SEC. 901. Title 28 of the United States Code, section 1447(d), is amended to read as follows:
"An order remanding a case to the State court from which it was removed is not reviewable on appeal or otherwise, except that an order remanding a case to the State court from which it was removed pursuant to section 1443 of this title shall be reviewable by appeal or otherwise."
SEC. 902. Whenever an action has been commenced in any court of the United States seeking relief from the denial of equal protection of the laws under the fourteenth amendment to the Constitution on account of race, color, religion, or national origin, the Attorney General for or in the name of the United States may intervene in such action upon timely application if the Attorney General certifies that the case is of general public importance. In such action the United States shall be entitled to the same relief as if it had instituted the action.

Title X –– Establishment of Community Relations Service

SEC. 1001. (a) There is hereby established in and as a part of the Department of Commerce a Community Relations Service (hereinafter referred to as the "Service"), which shall be headed by a Director who shall be appointed by the President with the advice and consent of the Senate for a term of four years. The Director is authorized to appoint, subject to the civil service laws and regulations, such other personnel as may be necessary to enable the Service to carry out its functions and duties, and to fix their compensation in accordance with the Classification Act of 1949, as amended. The Director is further authorized to procure services as authorized by section

15 of the Act of August 2, 1946 (60 Stat. 810; 5 U.S.C. 55(a)), but at rates for individuals not in excess of $75 per diem.

(b) Section 106(a) of the Federal Executive Pay Act of 1956, as amended (5 U.S.C. 2205(a)), is further amended by adding the following clause thereto:

"(52) Director, Community Relations Service."

SEC. 1002. It shall be the function of the Service to provide assistance to communities and persons therein in resolving disputes, disagreements, or difficulties relating to discriminatory practices based on race, color, or national origin which impair the rights of persons in such communities under the Constitution or laws of the United States or which affect or may affect interstate commerce. The Service may offer its services in cases of such disputes, disagreements, or difficulties whenever, in its judgment, peaceful relations among the citizens of the community involved are threatened thereby, and it may offer its services either upon its own motion or upon the request of an appropriate State or local official or other interested person.

SEC. 1003. (a) The Service shall, whenever possible, in performing its functions, seek and utilize the cooperation of appropriate State or local, public, or private agencies.

(b) The activities of all officers and employees of the Service in providing conciliation assistance shall be conducted in confidence and without publicity, and the Service shall hold confidential any information acquired in the regular performance of its duties upon the understanding that it would be so held. No officer or employee of the Service shall engage in the performance of investigative or prosecuting functions of any department or agency in any litigation arising out of a dispute in which he acted on behalf of the Service. Any officer or other employee of the Service, who shall make public in any manner whatever any information in violation of this subsection, shall be deemed guilty of a misdemeanor and, upon conviction thereof shall be fined not more than $1,000 or imprisoned not more than one year.

SEC. 1004. Subject to the provisions of sections 205 and 1003(b), the Director shall, on or before January 31 of each year, submit to the Congress a report of the activities of the Service during the preceding fiscal year.

The XI –– Miscellaneous

SEC. 1101. In any proceeding for criminal contempt arising under title II, III, IV, V VI, or VII of this Act, the accused, upon demand therefor, shall be entitled to a trial by jury, which shall conform as near as may be to the practice in criminal cases. Upon conviction, the accused shall not be fined more than $1,000 or imprisoned for more than six months.

This section shall not apply to contempts committed in the presence of the court, or so near thereto as to obstruct the administration of justice, nor to the misbehavior, misconduct, or disobedience of any officer of the court in respect to writs, orders, or process of the court. No person shall be convicted of criminal contempt hereunder unless the act or omission constituting such contempt shall have been intentional, as required in other cases of criminal contempt.

Nor shall anything herein be construed to deprive courts of their power, by civil contempt proceedings, without a jury, to secure compliance with or to prevent obstruction of, as distinguished from punishment for violations of, any lawful writ, process, order, rule, decree, or command of the court in accordance with the prevailing usages of law and equity, including the power of detention.

SEC. 1102. No person should be put twice in jeopardy under the laws of the United States for the same act or omission. For this reason, an acquittal or conviction in a prosecution for a specific crime under the laws of the United States shall bar a proceeding for criminal contempt, which is based upon the same act or omission and which arises under the provisions of this Act; and an acquittal or conviction in a proceeding for criminal contempt, which arises under the provisions of this Act, shall bar a prosecution for a specific crime under the laws of the United States based upon the same act or omission.

SEC. 1103. Nothing in this Act shall be construed to deny, impair, or otherwise affect any right or authority of the Attorney General or of the United States or any agency or officer thereof under existing law to institute or intervene in any action or proceeding.

SEC. 1104. Nothing contained in any title of this Act shall be construed as indicating an intent on the part of Congress to occupy the field in which any such title operates to the exclusion of State laws on the same subject matter, nor shall any provision of this Act be construed as invalidating any provision of State law unless such provision is inconsistent with any of the purposes of this Act, or any provision thereof.

SEC. 1105. There are hereby authorized to be appropriated such sums as are necessary to carry out the provisions of this Act.

SEC. 1106. If any provision of this Act or the application thereof to any person or circumstances is held invalid, the remainder of the Act and the application of the provision to other persons not similarly situated or to other circumstances shall not be affected thereby.

Approved July 2, 1964.

LESSON THIRTEEN

THE VOTING RIGHTS ACT

Voting Rights Act

(August 6, 1965)

United States Congress

▌The History[16*]

This "act to enforce the fifteenth amendment to the Constitution" was signed into law 95 years after the amendment was ratified. In those years, African Americans in the South faced tremendous obstacles to voting, including poll taxes, literacy tests, and other bureaucratic restrictions to deny them the right to vote. They also risked harassment, intimidation, economic reprisals, and physical violence when they tried to register or vote. As a result, very few African Americans were registered voters, and they had very little, if any, political power, either locally or nationally.

In 1964, numerous demonstrations were held, and the considerable violence that erupted brought renewed attention to the issue of voting rights. The murder of voting-rights activists in Mississippi and the attack by state troopers on peaceful marchers in Selma, Alabama, gained national attention and persuaded President Johnson and Congress to initiate meaningful and effective national voting rights legislation. The combination of public revulsion to the violence and Johnson's political skills stimulated Congress to pass the voting rights bill on August 5, 1965.

The legislation, which President Johnson signed into law the next day, outlawed literacy tests and provided for the appointment of Federal examiners (with the power to register qualified citizens to vote) in those jurisdictions that were "covered" according to a formula provided in the statute. In addition, Section 5 of the act required covered jurisdictions to obtain "preclearance" from either the District Court for the District of Columbia or the U.S. Attorney General for any new voting practices and procedures. Section 2, which closely followed the language of the 15th amendment, applied a nationwide prohibition of the denial or abridgment of the right to vote on account of race or color. The use of poll taxes in national elections had been abolished by the 24th amendment (1964) to the Constitution; the Voting Rights Act directed the Attorney General to challenge the use of poll taxes in state and local elections. *In Harper v. Virginia State Board of Elections*, 383 U.S. 663 (1966), the Supreme Court held Virginia's poll tax to be unconstitutional under the 14th amendment.

Because the Voting Rights Act of 1965 was the most significant statutory change in the relationship between the Federal and state governments in the area of voting since the Reconstruction period following the Civil War, it was immediately challenged in the courts. Between 1965 and 1969, the Supreme Court issued several key decisions upholding the constitutionality of Section

---

[16] * Originally published as "Voting Rights Act (1965)," *America's Historical Documents,* The National Archives, U.S. National Archives and Records Administration, College Park, Maryland, 2008. For additional information see "Voting Rights Act (1965)," *America's Historical Documents*, U.S. National Archives and Records Administration, College Park, Maryland, 2008. This agency is listed in the *National Resource Directory* section of this volume.

5 and affirming the broad range of voting practices for which preclearance was required. [See *South Carolina v. Katzenbach*, 383 U.S. 301, 327-28 (1966) and *Allen v. State Board of Elections*, 393 U.S. 544 (1969)].

The law had an immediate impact. By the end of 1965, a quarter of a million new black voters had been registered, one-third by Federal examiners. By the end of 1966, only 4 out of the 13 southern states had fewer than 50 percent of African Americans registered to vote. The Voting Rights Act of 1965 was readopted and strengthened in 1970, 1975, and 1982.

The Document

Voting Rights Act

AN ACT To enforce the fifteenth amendment to the Constitution of the United States, and for other purposes.

Be it enacted by the Senate and House of Representatives of the United States of America in Congress [p[17]*338] assembled, That this Act shall be known as the "Voting Rights Act of 1965."

SEC. 2. No voting qualification or prerequisite to voting, or standard, practice, or procedure shall be imposed or applied by any State or political subdivision to deny or abridge the right of any citizen of the United States to vote on account of race or color.

SEC. 3.

(a) Whenever the Attorney General institutes a proceeding under any statute to enforce the guarantees of the fifteenth amendment in any State or political subdivision the court shall authorize the appointment of Federal examiners by the United States Civil Service Commission in accordance with section 6 to serve for such period of time and for such political subdivisions as the court shall determine is appropriate to enforce the guarantees of the fifteenth amendment (1) as part of any interlocutory order if the court determines that the appointment of such examiners is necessary to enforce such guarantees or (2) as part of any final judgment if the court finds that violations of the fifteenth amendment justifying equitable relief have occurred in such State or subdivision: Provided, That the court need not authorize the appointment of examiners if any incidents of denial or abridgement of the right to vote on account of race or color (1) have been few in number and have been promptly and effectively corrected by State or local action, (2) the continuing effect of such incidents has been eliminated, and (3) there is no reasonable probability of their recurrence in the future. (b) If in a proceeding instituted by the Attorney General under any statute to enforce the guarantees of the fifteenth amendment in any State or political subdivision the court finds that a test or device has been used for the purpose or with the effect of denying or abridging the right of any citizen of the United States to vote on account of race or color, it shall suspend the use of [p*339] tests and devices in such State or political subdivisions as the court shall determine is appropriate and for such period as it deems necessary.

---

[17] *This chapter is based on a speech given by Robert M. Gates at the *World Forum on the Future of Democracy* held in Williamsburg, VA, on September 17, 2007. The entire speech is available on the U.S. Department of Defense website (http://www.defenselink.mil/)

(c) If in any proceeding instituted by the Attorney General under any statute to enforce the guarantees of the fifteenth amendment in any State or political subdivision the court finds that violations of the fifteenth amendment justifying equitable relief have occurred within the territory of such State or political subdivision, the court, in addition to such relief as it may grant, shall retain jurisdiction for such period as it may deem appropriate and during such period no voting qualification or prerequisite to voting, or standard, practice, or procedure with respect to voting different from that in force or effect at the time the proceeding was commenced shall be enforced unless and until the court finds that such qualification, prerequisite, standard, practice, or procedure does not have the purpose and will not have the effect of denying or abridging the right to vote on account of race or color: Provided, That such qualification, prerequisite, standard, practice, or procedure may be enforced if the qualification, prerequisite, standard, practice, or procedure has been submitted by the chief legal officer or other appropriate official of such State or subdivision to the Attorney General and the Attorney General has not interposed an objection within sixty days after such submission, except that neither the court's finding nor the Attorney General's failure to object shall bar a subsequent action to enjoin enforcement of such qualification, prerequisite, standard, practice, or procedure.

SEC. 4. (a) To assure that the right of citizens of the United States to vote is not denied or abridged on account of race or color, no citizen shall be denied the right to vote in any Federal, State, or local election because of his failure to comply with any test or device in any State with respect to which the determinations have been [p*340] made under subsection (b) or in any political subdivision with respect to which such determinations have been made as a separate unit, unless the United States District Court for the District of Columbia in an action for a declaratory judgment brought by such State or subdivision against the United States has determined that no such test or device has been used during the five years preceding the filing of the action for the purpose or with the effect of denying or abridging the right to vote on account of race or color: Provided, That no such declaratory judgment shall issue with respect to any plaintiff for a period of five years after the entry of a final judgment of any court of the United States, other than the denial of a declaratory judgment under this section, whether entered prior to or after the enactment of this Act, determining that denials or abridgments of the right to vote on account of race or color through the use of such tests or devices have occurred anywhere in the territory of such plaintiff. An action pursuant to this subsection shall be heard and determined by a court of three judges in accordance with the provisions of section 2284 of title 28 of the United States Code and any appeal shall lie to the Supreme Court. The court shall retain jurisdiction of any action pursuant to this subsection for five years after judgment and shall reopen the action upon motion of the Attorney General alleging that a test or device has been used for the purpose or with the effect of denying or abridging the right to vote on account of race or color.

If the Attorney General determines that he has no reason to believe that any such test or device has been used during the five years preceding the filing of the action for the purpose or with the effect of denying or abridging the right to vote on account of race or color, he shall consent to the entry of such judgment.

(b) The provisions of subsection (a) shall apply in any State or in any political subdivision of a state which (1) the Attorney General determines maintained on November 1, 1964, any test or device, and with respect to which (2) the Director of the Census determines that less than 50 percentum of the persons of voting age residing therein were registered on November 1, 1964, or that less than 50 percentum of such persons voted in the presidential election of November 1964.

A determination or certification of the Attorney General or of the Director of the Census under this section or under section 6 or section 13 shall not be reviewable in any court and shall be effective upon publication in the Federal Register.

(c) The phrase "test or device" shall mean any requirement that a person as a prerequisite for voting or registration for voting (1) demonstrate the ability to read, write, understand, or interpret any matter, (2) demonstrate any educational achievement or his knowledge of any particular subject, (3) possess good moral character, or (4) prove his qualifications by the voucher of registered voters or members of any other class.

(d) For purposes of this section no State or political subdivision shall be determined to have engaged in the use of tests or devices for the purpose or with the effect of denying or abridging the right to vote on account of race or color if (1) incidents of such use have been few in number and have been promptly and effectively corrected by State or local action, (2) the continuing effect of such incidents has been eliminated, and (3) there is no reasonable probability of their recurrence in the future.

(e)(1) Congress hereby declares that to secure the rights under the fourteenth amendment of persons educated in American-flag schools in which the predominant [p*342] classroom language was other than English, it is necessary to prohibit the States from conditioning the right to vote of such persons on ability to read, write, understand, or interpret any matter in the English language. (2) No person who demonstrates that he has successfully completed the sixth primary grade in a public school in, or a private school accredited by, any State or territory, the District of Columbia, or the Commonwealth of Puerto Rico in which the predominant classroom language was other than English, shall be denied the right to vote in any Federal, State, or local election because of his inability to read, write, understand, or interpret any matter in the English language, except that, in States in which State law provides that a different level of education is presumptive of literacy, he shall demonstrate that he has successfully completed an equivalent level of education in a public school in, or a private school accredited by, any State or territory, the District of Columbia, or the Commonwealth of Puerto Rico in which the predominant classroom language was other than English.

SEC. 5. Whenever a State or political subdivision with respect to which the prohibitions set forth in section 4(a) are in effect shall enact or seek to administer any voting qualification or prerequisite to voting, or standard, practice, or procedure with respect to voting different from that in force or effect on November 1, 1964, such State or subdivision may institute an action in the United States District Court for the District of Columbia for a declaratory judgment that such qualification, prerequisite, standard, practice, or procedure does not have the purpose and will not have the effect of denying or abridging the right to vote on account of race or color, and unless and until the court enters such judgment no person shall be denied the right to vote for failure to comply with such qualification, prerequisite, standard, practice, [p*343] or procedure:

Provided, That such qualification, prerequisite, standard, practice, or procedure may be enforced without such proceeding if the qualification, prerequisite, standard, practice, or procedure has been submitted by the chief legal officer or other appropriate official of such State or subdivision to the Attorney General and the Attorney General has not interposed an objection within sixty days after such submission, except that neither the Attorney General's failure to object nor a declaratory judgment entered under this section shall bar a subsequent action to enjoin enforcement of such qualification, prerequisite, standard, practice, or procedure. Any action under this section shall be heard and determined by a court of three judges in accordance with the provisions of section 2284 of title 28 of the United States Code and any appeal shall lie to the Supreme Court.

SEC. 6. Whenever (a) a court has authorized the appointment of examiners pursuant to the provisions of section 3(a), or (b) unless a declaratory judgment has been rendered under section 4(a), the Attorney General certifies with respect to any political subdivision named in, or included within the scope of, determinations made under section 4(b) that (1) he has received complaints in writing from twenty or more residents of such political subdivision alleging that they have been denied the right to vote under color of law on account of race or color, and that he believes such complaints to be meritorious, or (2) that, in his judgment (considering, among other factors, whether the ratio of nonwhite persons to white persons registered to vote within such subdivision appears to him to be reasonably attributable to violations of the fifteenth amendment or whether substantial evidence exists that bonafide efforts are being made within such subdivision to comply with the fifteenth amendment), the appointment of examiners is otherwise necessary to [p*344] enforce the guarantees of the fifteenth amendment, the Civil Service Commission shall appoint as many examiners for such subdivision as it may deem appropriate to prepare and maintain lists of persons eligible to vote in Federal, State, and local elections. Such examiners, hearing officers provided for in section 9(a), and other persons deemed necessary by the Commission to carry out the provisions and purposes of this Act shall be appointed, compensated, and separated without regard to the provisions of any statute administered by the Civil Service Commission, and service under this Act shall not be considered employment for the purposes of any statute administered by the Civil Service Commission, except the provisions of section 9 of the Act of August 2, 1939, as amended (5 U.S.C. 118i), prohibiting partisan political activity: Provided, That the Commission is authorized, after consulting the head of the appropriate department or agency, to designate suitable persons in the official service of the United States, with their consent, to serve in these positions. Examiners and hearing officers shall have the power to administer oaths.

SEC. 7.

(a) The examiners for each political subdivision shall, at such places as the Civil Service Commission shall by regulation designate, examine applicants concerning their qualifications for voting. An application to an examiner shall be in such form as the Commission may require and shall contain allegations that the applicant is not otherwise registered to vote.

(b) Any person whom the examiner finds, in accordance with instructions received under section 9(b), to have the qualifications prescribed by State law not inconsistent with the Constitution and laws of the United States shall promptly be placed on a list of eligible voters. A challenge to such listing may be made in accordance with section 9(a) and shall not be the basis for a prosecution under section 12 of this Act. The examiner [p*345] shall certify and transmit such list, and any supplements as appropriate, at least once a month, to the offices of the appropriate election officials, with copies to the Attorney General and the attorney general of the State, and any such lists and supplements thereto transmitted during the month shall be available for public inspection on the last business day of the month and, in any event, not later than the forty-fifth day prior to any election. The appropriate State or local election official shall place such names on the official voting list. Any person whose name appears on the examiner's list shall be entitled and allowed to vote in the election district of his residence unless and until the appropriate election officials shall have been notified that such person has been removed from such list in accordance with subsection (d): Provided, That no person shall be entitled to vote in any election by virtue of this Act unless his name shall have been certified and transmitted on such a list to the offices of the appropriate election officials at least forty-five days prior to such election.

(c) The examiner shall issue to each person whose name appears on such a list a certificate evidencing his eligibility to vote.

(d) A person whose name appears on such a list shall be removed therefrom by an examiner if (1) such person has been successfully challenged in accordance with the procedure prescribed in section 9, or (2) he has been determined by an examiner to have lost his eligibility to vote under State law nor inconsistent with the Constitution and the laws of the United States.

Sec. 8. Whenever an examiner is serving under this Act in any political subdivision, the Civil Service Commission may assign, at the request of the Attorney General, one or more persons, who may be officers of the United States, (1) to enter and attend at any place for holding an election in such subdivision for the purpose [p*346] of observing whether persons who are entitled to vote are being permitted to vote, and (2) to enter and attend at any place for tabulating the votes cast at any election held in such subdivision for the purpose of observing whether votes cast by persons entitled to vote are being properly tabulated. Such persons so assigned shall report to an examiner appointed for such political subdivision, to the Attorney General, and if the appointment of examiners has been authorized pursuant to section 3(a), to the court.

SEC. 9.

(a) Any challenge to a listing on an eligibility list prepared by an examiner shall be heard and determined by a hearing officer appointed by and responsible to the Civil Service Commission and under such rules as the Commission shall by regulation prescribe. Such challenge shall be entertained only if filed at such office within the State as the Civil Service Commission shall by regulation designate, and within ten days after the listing of the challenged person is made available for public inspection, and if supported by (1) the affidavits of at least two persons having personal knowledge of the facts constituting grounds for the challenge, and (2) a certification that a copy of the challenge and affidavits have been served by mail or in person upon the person challenged at his place of residence set out in the application. Such challenge shall be determined within fifteen days after it has been filed. A petition for review of the decision of the hearing officer may be filed in the United States court of appeals for the circuit in which the person challenged resides within fifteen days after service of such decision by mail on the person petitioning for review but no decision of a hearing officer shall be reversed unless clearly erroneous. Any person listed shall be entitled and allowed to vote pending final determination by the hearing officer and by the court [p*347].

(b) The times, places, procedures, and form for application and listing pursuant to this Act and removals from the eligibility lists shall be prescribed by regulations promulgated by the Civil Service Commission and the Commission shall, after consultation with the Attorney General, instruct examiners concerning applicable State law not inconsistent with the Constitution and laws of the United States with respect to (1) the qualifications required for listing, and (2) loss of eligibility to vote.

(c) Upon the request of the applicant or the challenger or on its own motion the Civil Service Commission shall have the power to require by subpoena the attendance and testimony of witnesses and the production of documentary evidence relating to any matter pending before it under the authority of this section. In case of contumacy or refusal to obey a subpoena, any district court of the United States or the United States court of any territory or possession, or the District Court of the United States for the District of Columbia, within the jurisdiction of which said person guilty of contumacy or refusal to obey is found or resides or is domiciled or transacts business, or has appointed an agent for receipt of service of process, upon application by the Attorney General of the United States shall have jurisdiction to issue to such person an order requiring such person to appear before the Commission or a hearing officer, there to produce pertinent, relevant, and nonprivileged documentary evidence if so ordered, or there to give testimony touching the matter under investigation, and any failure to obey such order of the court may be punished by said court as a contempt thereof.

SEC. 10. (a) The Congress finds that the requirement of the payment of a poll tax as a precondition to voting (i) precludes persons of limited means from voting or imposes unreasonable financial hardship upon such persons [p*348] as a precondition to their exercise of the franchise, (ii) does not bear a reasonable relationship to any legitimate State interest in the conduct of elections, and (iii) in some areas has the purpose or effect of denying persons the right to vote because of race or color. Upon the basis of these findings, Congress declares that the constitutional right of citizens to vote is denied or abridged in some areas by the requirement of the payment of a poll tax as a precondition to voting. (b) In the exercise of the powers of Congress under section 5 of the fourteenth amendment and section 2 of the fifteenth amendment, the Attorney General is authorized and directed to institute forthwith in the name of the United States such actions, including actions against States or political subdivisions, for declaratory judgment or injunctive relief against the enforcement of any requirement of the payment of a poll tax as a precondition to voting, or substitute therefor enacted after November 1, 1964, as will be necessary to implement the declaration of subsection (a) and the purposes of this section.

(c) The district courts of the United States shall have jurisdiction of such actions which shall be heard and determined by a court of three judges in accordance with the provisions of section 2284 of title 28 of the United States Code and any appeal shall lie to the Supreme Court. It shall be the duty of the judges designated to hear the case to assign the case for hearing at the earliest practicable date, to participate in the hearing and determination thereof, and to cause the case to be in every way expedited.

(d) During the pendency of such actions, and thereafter if the courts, notwithstanding this action by the Congress, should declare the requirement of the payment of a poll tax to be constitutional, no citizen of the United States who is a resident of a State or political [p*349] subdivision with respect to which determinations have been made under subsection 4(b) and a declaratory judgment has not been entered under subsection 4(a), during the first year he becomes otherwise entitled to vote by reason of registration by State or local officials or listing by an examiner, shall be denied the right to vote for failure to pay a poll tax if he tenders payment of such tax for the current year to an examiner or to the appropriate State or local official at least forty-five days prior to election, whether or not such tender would be timely or adequate under State law. An examiner shall have authority to accept such payment from any person authorized by this Act to make an application for listing, and shall issue a receipt for such payment. The examiner shall transmit promptly any such poll tax payment to the office of the State or local official authorized to receive such payment under State law, together with the name and address of the applicant.

SEC. 11. (a) No person acting under color of law shall fail or refuse to permit any person to vote who is entitled to vote under any provision of this Act or is otherwise qualified to vote, or willfully fail or refuse to tabulate, count, and report such person's vote. (b) No person, whether acting under color of law or otherwise, shall intimidate, threaten, or coerce, or attempt to intimidate, threaten, or coerce any person for voting or attempting to vote, or intimidate, threaten, or coerce, or attempt to intimidate, threaten, or coerce any person for urging or aiding any person to vote or attempt to vote, or intimidate, threaten, or coerce any person for exercising any powers or duties under section 3(a), 6, 8, 9, 10, or 12(e).

(c) Whoever knowingly or willfully gives false information as to his name, address, or period of residence in the voting district for the purpose of establishing his eligibility to register or vote, or conspires with another [p*350] individual for the purpose of encouraging his false registration to vote or illegal voting, or pays or offers to pay or accepts payment either for registration to vote or for voting shall be fined not more than $10,000 or imprisoned not more than five years, or both: Provided, however, That this provision shall be applicable only to general, special, or primary elections held solely or in part for the purpose of selecting or electing any candidate for the office of President, Vice President, presidential elector, Member of the United States Senate, Member of the United States House of Representatives, or Delegates or Commissioners from the territories or possessions, or Resident Commissioner of the Commonwealth of Puerto Rico.

(d) Whoever, in any matter within the jurisdiction of an examiner or hearing officer knowingly and willfully falsifies or conceals a material fact, or makes any false, fictitious, or fraudulent statements or representations, or makes or uses any false writing or document knowing the same to contain any false, fictitious, or fraudulent statement or entry, shall be fined not more than $10,000 or imprisoned not more than five years, or both.

SEC. 12. (a) Whoever shall deprive or attempt to deprive any person of any right secured by section 2, 3, 4, 5, 7, or 10 or shall violate section 11(a) or (b), shall be fined not more than $5,000, or imprisoned not more than five years, or both. (b) Whoever, within a year following an election in a political subdivision in which an examiner has been appointed (1) destroys, defaces, mutilates, or otherwise alters the marking of a paper ballot which has been cast in such election, or (2) alters any official record of voting in such election tabulated from a voting machine or otherwise, shall be fined not more than. $5,000, or imprisoned not more than five years, or both [p*351].

(c) Whoever conspires to violate the provisions of subsection (a) or (b) of this section, or interferes with any right secured by section 2, 3, 4, 5, 7, 10, or 11(a) or (b) shall be fined not more than $5,000, or imprisoned not more than five years, or both.

(d) Whenever any person has engaged or there are reasonable grounds to believe that any person is about to engage in any act or practice prohibited by section 2, 3, 4, 5, 7, 10, 11, or subsection (b) of this section, the Attorney General may institute for the United States, or in the name of the United States, an action for preventive relief, including an application for a temporary or permanent injunction, restraining order, or other order, and including an order directed to the State and State or local election officials to require them (1) to permit persons listed under this Act to vote and (2) to count such votes.

(e) Whenever in any political subdivision in which there are examiners appointed pursuant to this Act any persons allege to such an examiner within forty-eight hours after the closing of the polls that notwithstanding (1) their listing under this Act or registration by an appropriate election official and (2) their eligibility to vote, they have not been permitted to vote in such election, the examiner shall forthwith notify the Attorney General if such allegations in his opinion appear to be well founded. Upon receipt of such notification, the Attorney General may forthwith file with the district court an application for an order providing for the marking, casting, and counting of the ballots of such persons and requiring the inclusion of their votes in the total vote before the results of such election shall be deemed final and any force or effect given thereto. The district court shall hear and determine such matters immediately after the filing of such application. The remedy provided [p*352] in this subsection shall not preclude any remedy available under State or Federal law.

(f) The district courts of the United States shall have jurisdiction of proceedings instituted pursuant to this section and shall exercise the same without regard to whether a person asserting rights under the provisions of this Act shall have exhausted any administrative or other remedies that may be provided by law.

SEC. 13. Listing procedures shall be terminated in any political subdivision of any State (a) with respect to examiners appointed pursuant to clause (b) of section 6 whenever the Attorney General notifies the Civil Service Commission, or whenever the District Court for the District of Columbia determines in an action for declaratory judgment brought by any political subdivision with respect to which the Director of the Census has determined that more than 50 percentum of the nonwhite persons of voting age residing therein are registered to vote, (1) that all persons listed by an examiner for such subdivision have been placed on the appropriate voting registration roll, and (2) that there is no longer reasonable cause to believe that persons will be deprived of or denied the right to vote on account of race or color in such subdivision, and (b), with respect to examiners appointed pursuant to section 3(a), upon order of the authorizing court. A political subdivision may petition the Attorney General for the termination of listing procedures under clause (a) of this section, and may petition the Attorney General to request the Director of the

Census to take such survey or census as may be appropriate for the making of the determination provided for in this section. The District Court for the District of Columbia shall have jurisdiction to require such survey or census to be made by the Director of the Census and it shall require him to do so if it deems the Attorney [p*353] General's refusal to request such survey or census to be arbitrary or unreasonable.

SEC. 14.

(a) All cases of criminal contempt arising under the provisions of this Act shall be governed by section 151 of the Civil Rights Act of 1957 (42 U.S.C. 1995). (b) No court other than the District Court for the District of Columbia or a court of appeals in any proceeding under section 9 shall have jurisdiction to issue any declaratory judgment pursuant to section 4 or section 5 or any restraining order or temporary or permanent injunction against the execution or enforcement of any provision of this Act or any action of any Federal officer or employee pursuant hereto.

(c) (1) The terms "vote" or "voting" shall include all action necessary to make a vote effective in any primary, special, or general election, including, but not limited to, registration, listing pursuant to this Act, or other action required by law prerequisite to voting, casting a ballot, and having such ballot counted properly and included in the appropriate totals of votes cast with respect to candidates for public or party office and propositions for which votes are received in an election. (2) The term "political subdivision" shall mean any county or parish, except that, where registration for voting is not conducted under the supervision of a county or parish, the term shall include any other subdivision of a State which conducts registration for voting.

(d) In any action for a declaratory judgment brought pursuant to section 4 or section 5 of this Act. subpoenas for witnesses who are required to attend the District Court for the District of Columbia may be served in any judicial district of the United States: Provided, That no writ of subpoena shall issue for witnesses without the District of Columbia at a greater distance than one hundred [p*354] miles from the place of holding court without the permission of the District Court for the District of Columbia being first had upon proper application and cause shown.

SEC. 15. Section 2004 of the Revised Statutes (42 U.S.C. 1971), as amended by section 131 of the Civil Rights Act of 1957 (71 Stat. 637), and amended by section 601 of the Civil Rights Act of 1960 (74 Stat. 90), and as further amended by section 101 of the Civil Rights Act of 1964 (78 Stat. 241), is further amended as follows:

(a) Delete the word "Federal" wherever it appears in subsections (a) and (c); (b) Repeal subsection (f) and designate the present subsections (g) and (h) as (f) and (g), respectively.

SEC. 16. The Attorney General and the Secretary of Defense, jointly, shall make a full and complete study to determine whether, under the laws or practices of any State or States, there are preconditions to voting, which might tend to result in discrimination against citizens serving in the Armed Forces of the United States seeking to vote. Such officials shall, jointly, make a report to the Congress not later than June 30, 1966, containing the results of such study, together with a list of any States in which such preconditions exist, and shall include in such report such recommendations for legislation as they deem advisable to prevent discrimination in voting against citizens serving in the Armed Forces of the United States.

SEC. 17. Nothing in this Act shall be construed to deny, impair, or otherwise adversely affect the right to vote of any person registered to vote under the law of any State or political subdivision.

SEC. 18. There are hereby authorized to be appropriated such sums as are necessary to carry out the provisions of this Act [p*355].

SEC 19. If any provision of this Act or the application thereof to any person or circumstances is held invalid, the remainder of the Act and the application of the provision to other persons not similarly situated or to other circumstances shall not be affected thereby.

Approved August 6, 1965.

THE FUTURE

The Future of Democracy

Robert M. Gates

Senator Warner is a special friend. He has introduced me to the United States Senate for confirmation four times. The first time was more than 20 years ago. And that dates us both. He is a great Virginian, a great American, and we will certainly all miss him when he brings his remarkable career in public service to a close next year.

I want to thank Justice Sandra Day O'Connor, one of the most distinguished jurists and public servants in America, for inviting me today. It was Justice O'Connor who administered my oath of office as Director of Central Intelligence in 1991. And last year we served together on the Baker-Hamilton Commission. Little did I know that my sojourn to Iraq a little over a year ago with the group would be only the first of many such visits for me.

Justice O'Connor and I share something else in common —— a love of the College of William and Mary, where she is currently the chancellor. And of course, it was a special pleasure to see her four months ago when I had the honor of giving the commencement address at my alma mater. Attending college here in Williamsburg shaped my love of history and my belief that public service is a vital component of a working democracy —— and of a meaningful life.

This setting is fitting for my topic today: a "realist's" view of promoting democracy abroad.

I had quite a reputation as a pessimist when I was in the intelligence business. A journalist once described me as the Eeyore of national security —— able to find the darkest cloud in any silver lining. I used to joke that when an intelligence officer smelled the flowers, he'd look around for the coffin. Today, as one looks around the world —— wars in Iraq and Afghanistan, an ambitious and fanatical theocracy in Iran, a nuclear North Korea, terrorism, and more —— there would seem to be ample grounds to be gloomy.

But there is a different perspective if we step back and look at the world through a wider lens —— a perspective that shows a dramatic growth in human freedom and democracy in just the time since this fall's college freshmen were born. Since 1989, hundreds of millions of people —— from Eastern and Central Europe and the former Soviet Union, to South Africa, Afghanistan, Iraq, and elsewhere —— have been liberated: they have left the darkness of despotism and walked into the bright sunshine of freedom.

Many have seized the opportunity, and freedom has prospered and strengthened; others liberated from the yoke of tyrannical ideologies or dictators continue to struggle to fully realize the dream. At no time in history, though, has freedom come to so many in so short a time. And in every case, the United States, overtly or covertly, in large ways or small, played a role in their liberation.

Still, we Americans continue to wrestle with the appropriate role this country should play in advancing freedom and democracy in the world. It was a source of friction through the entire Cold War. In truth, it has been a persistent question for this country throughout our history: How should we incorporate America's democratic ideals and aspirations into our relations with the rest of the world? And in particular, when to, and whether to try to change the way other nations govern themselves? Should America's mission to make the world "safe for democracy," as Woodrow Wilson said, or, in the words of John Quincy Adams, should America be "the well-wisher of freedom and independence of all" but the "champion and indicator only of our own"?

During my time today, I'd like to put this question and its associated debates in some historical context — a context I hope might help inform the difficult policy choices our nation faces today.

Let me first speak to geography — this place we are in.

It is a strange quirk of history that a backwoods outpost in an unexplored corner of America would hold in it the seeds of a global movement toward liberty and self-governance — toward the democratic institutions that underpin the free nations of the world and give hope to countless people in many others.

So much of what defines America first took root here in Virginia along the banks of the James River. When you think about it, the initial impetus for these institutions owed as much to the struggle for survival as to anything else. The challenges were myriad: along with disease, hunger, and war, the settlers faced no small number of divisions and discord. Four hundred years removed from those early days, it is all too easy to forget about these stormy beginnings.

The revolution that brought about this nation was similarly chaotic. As my distinguished William and Mary classmate, the historian Joe Ellis, wrote in his book, *Founding Brothers*, "No one present at the start knew how it would turn out in the end. What in retrospect has the look of a foreordained unfolding of God's will was in reality an improvisational affair in which sheer chance, pure luck — both good and bad — and specific decisions made in the crucible of specific military and political crises determined the outcome." Ellis further wrote "the real drama of the American Revolution ... was its inherent messiness. This ... exciting but terrifying sense that all the major players had at the time — namely, that they were making it up as they went along, improvising on the edge of catastrophe." We would do well to be mindful of the turbulence of our own early history as we contemplate the challenges facing contemporary fledgling democracies struggling to find their footing.

When I retired from government in 1993, it seemed that the success and spread of democracy was inexorable, a foregone conclusion — that with the collapse of the Soviet Union, the evolution of political systems had reached, in the words of one scholar at the time, the "end of history." But the relative calm in the immediate aftermath of the Cold War served only to mask new threats to the security of democratic nations: ethnic conflicts, new genocides, the proliferation of weapons of mass destruction — especially by rogue states and, above all, a new, more formidable, and more malignant form of terrorism embraced by Islamic extremists.

These new threats, and in particular, the conflicts in Iraq and Afghanistan, and the wider challenge of dealing with radical jihadist movements since September 11th, once again have people talking about the competing impulses in U.S. foreign policy: realism versus idealism, freedom versus security, values versus interests.

This is not a new debate. Not long after winning our own independence, the U.S. was faced with how to respond to the French Revolution — an issue that consumed the politics of the country during the 1790s. The issue was whether to support the revolutionary government and its war against an alliance of European monarchies led by Great Britain. To many, like Thomas

Jefferson, the French Revolution, with its stated ideals of liberty, equality, and fraternity, seemed a natural successor to our own. Jefferson wrote that "this ball of liberty. I believe most piously, is now so well in motion that it will roll round the globe."

John Adams and the Federalists, however, were just as adamantly opposed. They were appalled by the revolution's excesses and feared the spread of violent French radicalism to our shores. In fact, they accused the Jeffersonians of being "pimps of France," who "represented cutthroats who walk in rags." The Federalists mocked Jefferson for his rhetorical defense of freedom and equality across the Atlantic while he continued to own slaves. Adams and Alexander Hamilton were, in turn, accused of being crypto-monarchists.

It was left to President George Washington to resolve the matter. He had said that: "My best wishes are irresistibly excited whensoever, in any country, I see an oppressed nation unfurl the banners of freedom." But the European wars and, in particular, our estrangement from the British, had begun to disrupt the lives of ordinary Americans by impeding trade and causing riots and refugees. Washington, understanding the fragility of America's position at the time, adopted a neutrality policy towards France and would go on to make a peace treaty with Great Britain — sparking massive protests and accusations of selling out the spirit of 1776.

Consider the great historic irony: The United States had recently broken free of the British monarchy only with the help of an absolutist French king. Yet when France itself turned in the direction of popular rule and was confronted by Europe's monarchies, the United States took a pass and made amends with our old British foe.

In short, from our earliest days, America's leaders have struggled with "realistic" versus "idealistic" approaches to the international challenges facing us. The most successful leaders, starting with Washington, have steadfastly encouraged the spread of liberty, democracy, and human rights. At the same time, however, they have fashioned policies blending different approaches with different emphases in different places and different times.

Over the last century, we have allied with tyrants to defeat other tyrants. We have sustained diplomatic relations with governments even as we supported those attempting their overthrow.

We have at times made human rights the centerpiece of our national strategy even as we did business with some of the worst violators of human rights. We have worked with authoritarian governments to advance our own security interests even while urging them to reform.

We have used our military to eliminate governments seen as a threat to our national security, to undo aggression, to end ethnic slaughter, and to prevent chaos. In recent times, we have done this in Grenada, Panama, Kuwait, the Balkans, Haiti, Afghanistan, and Iraq. In the process, we have brought the possibility of democracy and freedom to tens of millions more who had been oppressed or were suffering.

To win and protect our own freedom, the United States has made common cause with countries that were far from free — from Louis XVI, to one of history's true monsters, Joseph Stalin. Without the one there is no American independence. Without the other, no end to the Third Reich. It is neither hypocrisy nor cynicism to believe fervently in freedom while adopting different approaches to advancing freedom at different times along the way — including temporarily making common cause with despots to defeat greater or more urgent threats to our freedom or interests.

The consuming goal for most of my professional life was containing the threat of the Soviet Union and seeing a Europe made whole and free. For most of the Cold War, the ideal surely seemed distant, even unreachable. One prominent columnist wrote in *Time* magazine in 1982 that "it would be wishful thinking to predict that international Communism someday will either self-destruct or so exhaust itself."

During that struggle, as for most of our history, inspiring presidential rhetoric about freedom, along with many firm stands for human rights and self-determination, had to coexist with often grubby compromises and marriages of convenience that were necessary to stave off the Evil Empire.

But the Western democracies —— joined as the Atlantic Alliance —— came together to get the big things right. The democracies' shared belief in political and economic freedom and religious tolerance was the glue that held us fast despite the many quarrels along the way.

President Bush said in his second inaugural address, "[I]t is the policy of the United States to seek and support the growth of democratic movements and institutions in every nation and culture, with the ultimate goal of ending tyranny in our world."

When we discuss openly our desire for democratic values to take hold across the globe, we are describing a world that may be many years or decades off. Though achievement of the ideal may be limited by time, space, resources, or human nature, we must not allow ourselves to discard or disparage the ideal itself. It is vital that we speak out about what we believe and let the world know where we stand. It is vital that we give hope and aid to those who seek freedom.

I still remember working on the advance team for President Ford when he attended the Helsinki conference in 1975. Many critics were opposed to America's participation, since they believed that the accords did little but ratify the Soviet Union's takings in Eastern and Central Europe. The treaty's provisions on human rights were disparaged as little more than window dressing. However, the conference and treaty represent another of history's ironies. The Soviets demanded the conference for decades, finally got it, and it helped destroy them from the inside. We "realists" opposed holding the conference for decades, and attended grudgingly. We were wrong. For the meeting played a key role in our winning the Cold War.

Why? Because the human-rights provisions of the treaty made a moral statement whose significance was not lost on the dissidents behind the Iron Curtain. Helsinki became a spur for action, a rallying cry to fight tyranny from within and plant democracy in its place.

Vaclav Havel later said that the accords were a "shield, a chance to resist coercion and make it more difficult for the forces of coercion to retaliate." Lech Walesa called it a turning point "on the road to change in Gdansk."

President Carter's promotion of the spirit of Helsinki —— his elevation of human rights —— for the first time in the Cold War denied the Soviet Union the respect and the legitimacy it craved. Ronald Reagan's muscular words —— labeling the U.S.S.R. the "Evil Empire" and demanding that Mr. Gorbachev tear down that wall —— combined with his muscular defense policies hastened the implosion of the Soviet system.

Did these policies reflect hard-edged realism or lofty idealism? Both, actually. Were they implemented to defend our interests or to spread our democratic values? Again, both.

An underlying theme of American history is that we are compelled to defend our security and our interests in ways that, in the long run, lead to the spread of democratic values and institutions.

Since September 11th, these questions, contradictions, and dilemmas have taken on new urgency and presented new challenges for decision-makers, especially in an information age where every flaw and inconsistency — in words or deeds — is highlighted, magnified, and disseminated around the globe.

And, as with the Cold War, every action we take sends a signal about the depth of our strength and resolve. For our friends and allies, as well as our enemies and potential adversaries, our commitment to democratic values must be matched by actions.

Consider Afghanistan. The democracies of the West and our partners are united in the desire to see stability and decent government take hold in a land that was not only Al Queda's base of operation, but also home to one of the most oppressive governments in the world. And yet, though there is little doubt about the justness, necessity, and legitimacy of the Afghanistan mission, even though we agree that democracy is key to enduring stability there, many Allies are reluctant to provide the necessary resources and put their men and women in the line of fire.

Afghanistan is, in a very real sense, a litmus test of whether an alliance of advanced democracies can still make sacrifices and meet commitments to advance democracy. It would be a mark of shame on all of us if an alliance built on the foundation of democratic values were to falter at the very moment that it tries to lay that foundation for democracy elsewhere — especially in a mission that is crucial to our own security.

Likewise, for America to leave Iraq and the Middle East in chaos would betray and demoralize our allies there and in the region, while emboldening our most dangerous adversaries. To abandon an Iraq where just two years ago 12 million people quite literally risked their lives to vote for a constitutional democracy would be an offense to our interests as well as our values, a setback for the cause of freedom as well as the goal of stability.

Americans have never been a patient people. Today, we look at Russia, China, Afghanistan, Iraq, and others — and wonder at their excruciatingly slow progress toward democratic institutions and the rule of law.

The eminent French historian Helene Carrere d'Encausse wrote in 1992: "Reforms, when they go against the political traditions of the centuries, cannot be imposed in a hurry merely by enshrining them in the law. It takes time, and generally they are accompanied by violence." She added: "Reforms that challenge centuries of social relations based on ... the exclusion of the majority of society from the political process, are too profound to be readily accepted by those who have to pay the price of reform, even if they are seen to be indispensable. Reforms need time to develop ... It is this time that reformers have often lacked."

For more than 60 years, from Germany and Japan to South Korea, the Balkans, Haiti, Afghanistan, and Iraq, we and our allies have provided reformers — those who seek a free and democratic society — with time for their efforts to take hold. We must be realists and recognize that the institutions that underpin an enduring free society can only take root over time.

It is our country's tragedy, and our glory, that the tender shoots of freedom around the world for so many decades have been so often nourished with American blood. The spread of liberty both manifests our ideals and protects our interests –– in making the world "safe for democracy," we are also the "champion and vindicator" of our own. In reality, 'Wilson and Adams must coexist.

Throughout more than two centuries, the United States has made its share of mistakes. From time to time, we have strayed from our ideals and have been arrogant in dealing with others. Yet, what has brought us together with our democratic allies is a shared belief that the future of democracy and its spread is worth our enduring labors and sacrifices –– reflecting both our interests and our ideals.

I would like to close by returning to this corner of Virginia. In September 1796, shortly before George Washington left office, he addressed in his farewell statement an American people who had passed through the dangerous fires of war and revolution to form a union that was far from "perfect," but was a historic accomplishment nonetheless. He told them: "You have, in common cause, fought and triumphed together; the independence and liberty you possess are the work of joint councils and joint efforts, of common dangers, sufferings, and successes."

In this historic place, among old friends and new, let us take time to reflect on the common causes in which we have fought and triumphed together –– to protect our own liberty, and to extend its blessings to others. As we prepare for the challenges ahead, let us never forget that together we will face common dangers, sufferings, and successes –– but with confidence that, together, we will continue to protect that tender shoot of liberty first planted in this place so long ago.

At the time this was written, Robert M. Gates was Secretary of Defense, Defense Department, U.S. Government, Washington, D.C. He was originally appointed by President Bush, and was asked to reman in this position by President Obama.

APPENDICES

A. Glossary of Terms

Following is a list of terms commonly used to describe city, county, regional, state, and federal governments, and the actions taken by their public officials.

Abolish To do away with; to put an end to.

Act Legislation which has passed both Houses of Congress, approved by the President, or passed over his veto thus becoming law. Also used technically for a bill that has been passed by one House and engrossed.

Adjourn To stop or interrupt a meeting or session for a certain length of time.

Amendment A proposal by a Member (in committee or floor session of the respective Chamber) to alter the language or provisions of a bill or act. It is voted on in the same manner as a bill.

Appeal A request for a new hearing with a higher court.

Appellate Court A court which has the power to hear appeals and reverse court decisions.

Appointed Officials Public officials appointed by elected officials. These officials typically include an organization's top management staff (that is, chief executive and department managers).

Appointment An office or position for which one is chosen, not elected.

Appropriation A formal approval to draw funds from the Treasury for specific purposes. This may occur through an annual appropriations act, an urgent or supplemental appropriations act, a continuing resolution, or a permanent basis.

At-large Elections An election system where candidates are elected on a city-wide basis.

Authorization A law creating or sustaining a program, delegating power to implement it, and outlining its funding. Following authorization, an appropriation actually, draws funds from the Treasury.

Bill A proposed law which is being considered for approval.

Bipartisanship Cooperation between Members of both political parties in addressing a particular issue or proposal. Bipartisan action usually results when party leaders agree that an issue is of sufficient national importance as to preclude normal considerations of partisan advantage.

Board of Supervisors Typical name for the members of a governing body of county.

Boards and Commissions Typical names given to advisory bodies, appointed by the members of a governing body, to advise them on matters of importance in one of the many functional areas of government.

Calendar A list of bills, resolutions, or other matters to be considered before committees or on the floor of either House of Congress.

Campaign An attempt to convince people to vote for someone for public office.

Candidate A person seeking to obtain an office or position.

Census An official count of the population.

Charter A written grant which establishes a local government corporation or other institution, and defines its purposes and privileges.

Checks and Balances System of government which maintains balance of power among the branches of the government. Sets limits on the power of each branch. Sets up ways for each branch to correct any misuses of power by the other branches.

Citizen Participation Strategies have greater legitimacy and are easier to implement politically when the citizens served by a governmental entity feel that their interests and issues have been properly addressed during the planning process.

City Council Typical name for the members of a governing body of a municipality.

City Manager The Chief Executive Officer of a municipality.

Civil Relating to the rights of individuals, such as property and personal freedoms. Also, court cases which are not criminal.

Civil Rights Rights which belong to a person because of his or her being a member of a particular society, for example, an American.

Combination Elections A hybrid election system where some candidates are elected on a citywide basis, while other candidates are elected from a district, or ward.

Committee A group of people officially chosen to investigate or discuss a particular issue.

Compromise To settle differences by accepting less than what was wanted.

Constraint Limitation; restriction.

Contradict To conflict with; to oppose.

Controversial Relating to issues about which people have and express opposing views.

Cost/Benefit Analysis The relationship between economic benefits and cost associated with the operation of the department or program under study. The cost/benefit analysis may include both direct and indirect benefits and costs. Such analysis typically result in a payback period on initial investment.

Cost Center The smallest practical breakdown of expenditure and income into a grouping which will facilitate performance review, service evaluation, and the setting of priorities for particular activity or service area. Typically, it includes apportion of a single program within a department.

County Manager The Chief Executive Officer of a county government.

Cross Impact Analysis An analytical technique for identifying the various impacts of specific events or well-defined policy actions on other events. It explores whether the occurrence of one event or implementation of one policy is likely to inhibit, enhance, or have no effect on the occurrence of another event.

Criminal Relating to court cases in which a person has been accused of committing an action that is harmful to the public, such as murder or burglary.

Debate To discuss reasons for and against an issue or idea.

Delegate To grant or assign responsibility to another, to authorize a person or persons to represent the rest of the people.

Direct Democracy The people vote to make all of the decisions about their government.

Discrimination Being treated differently, usually worse, for some characteristic such as race, religion, national origin or sex. Discrimination is discouraged in the U.S.

District Elections An election system where candidates are elected from a district, or ward.

Econometric Model Forecasting technique that involves a system of interdependent regression equations that describe some sector of economic sales or profit activity. The parameters of the regression equations are usually estimated simultaneously. This technique better expresses the casualties involved than an ordinary regression equation.

Effectiveness Performing the right tasks correctly, consistent with a program's mission, goals, and objectives, or work plan. Relates to correctness and accuracy, not the efficiency of the program or tasks performed. Effectiveness alone is not an accurate measure of total productivity.

Efficiency Operating a program or performing work task economically. Relates to dollars spent or saved, not to the effectiveness of the program or task performed. Efficiency alone is not an accurate measure of total productivity.

Elected Officials Those public officials that hold elective office for a specified time period, typically called a term of office.

Environmental Scanning Process of identifying major environmental factors, events, or trends that impact, directly or indirectly, the organization and its internal operating systems. It is one of the initial steps in undertaking a strategic planning process.

Evaluation Systematic review of the mission, goals, objectives, and work plan for the organization and its various components. Evaluation occurs most frequently at the operational level by reviewing organizational objectives. The evaluation process typically results in the preparation of recommendation for needed adjustments.

Executive Person or group of persons responsible for governmental affairs and enforcement of laws.

Executive Director The title frequently used for the Chief Executive Officer of a regional government agency.

Exempt Free or excused from a requirement or duty.

External Environment All relevant elements or forces (for example, social, economic, political, and technological) external to, and having an impact on, the organization and its various components. Includes those forces that are not under the direct control of management.

Forecasting Techniques Methods (for example, qualitative, quantitative, and causal) used to project trends and predict future events or courses of action. Forecasting is an essential component of the strategic planning process. It may be used to analyze the external environment or to project organizational capabilities.

Foreign Policy The way a country treats and relates to the other countries of the world.

Forms of County Government Major forms include Commission, Commission-Administrator, and Council-Executive.

Forms of Municipal Government Major forms include Council-Manager, Mayor-Council, Commission, and Strong Mayor.

General Election A voting process involving most or all areas of the nation or state.

General Purpose Local Governments Includes cities and counties, since they both provide a wide range of services to the citizens they serve.

Gerrymandering Drawing of district lines to maximize the electoral advantage of political party or faction. The term was first used in 1812, when Elbridge Gerry was Governor of Massachusetts, to characterize the State redistricting plan.

Governor The Chief Executive Officer of a state government.

Hierarchical Ordered by rank or authority.

Hierarchy The order in which authority is ranked.

Impeach To charge a public official with committing a crime.

Inaugurate To place in office by a formal ceremony.

Influence The power to produce or cause an effect; to have an effect upon.

Inherent Rights Essential, basic rights.

Intergovernmental Relations The relationships between public officials at the various levels of government, most often dictated by legislation (e.g., grant requirements).

Internal Environment Relevant elements or forces (e.g., personnel, financial, communications, authority relationships, and management operating systems) internal to, and having an impact on, the operation of the organization and its various components. Includes those forces that are under the direct control of management.

Issue Trend, set of elements, or event which a group decides is important for policy-making purposes.

Issues Management Attempt to manage those issues that are important to an organization. These issues typically surface after the completion of an environmental scanning process, or other practice, leading to the identification of important issues. The issues identified should fall within the scope and purpose of the organization.

Jury A group of people chosen to hear a case in court. The *jury* makes a decision based upon the evidence.

Lame Duck Session A session of Congress meeting after elections have been held, but before the newly elected Congress has convened.

Law In municipal and county government this takes the form of an ordinance, which must be passed by majority vote of the governing body and published in a newspaper of general circulation.

Legislation The act or procedure of making laws; a law or laws made by such a procedure.

Levy To collect, a tax, for example.

Life-Cycle Analysis Involves an analysis and forecasting of new product or service growth rates based on S-curves. The phases of product or service acceptance by various groups are central to this analytical technique.

Line Personnel in those departments charged with responsibility for those functions necessary for the day-to-day performance of the organization. Includes those departments that directly produce goods and/or services to satisfy an organization's marketplace.

Line of Succession Order to succession.

Long-Range Planning Includes a planning process that commences with analyzing the internal organization and projecting current trends into the future for selected organizational components. This planning process may not include an assessment of an organization's external environment. It may be product or service oriented. This term should not be confused with strategic planning.

Management Consists basically of two types—strategic and operational. Strategic management is performed at the top of an organization's hierarchy; everything else is operational management. Operational management is organized along functional lines of responsibility. Strategic management sets direction for the organization, and operational management ensures that this direction is implemented.

Management Information System Integrated information system designed to provide strategic, tactical, and operational information to management. Usually involves periodic written or computer-generated reports which are timely, concise, and meaningful.

Management Operating System Formal system of linkages between different components of the organization by which the various departments communicate with each other and by which management directs the operation and receives information on its performance.

Mayor Typical name for the highest elective office in municipality.

Mission Statement of the role, or purpose, by which an organization plans to serve society. Mission statements may be set for different organizational components or departments. A department usually has only one mission statement.

Municipal The smallest unit of local government in the U.S.

Negotiate To discuss and then compromise on an issue to reach an agreement.

Nonprofit Organization Sometimes referred to as the third sector–the other two being the public and private sectors. Nonprofit organizations generally serve a public purpose and do not generate revenues beyond their operating expenses.

Objectives Tasks which are deemed necessary for an organization, or its components and departments, to achieve its goals. Several detailed objectives are typically set forth for each goal statement. Objectives include the operational implementation of goals.

Operational Issues Issues that relate to the internal operations of an organization such as finance, budgeting, personnel, and technology, to name a few. Operational issues may or may not relate to an organization's external environment and may not be of strategic importance to an organization.

Operational Management Tasks performed by line managers dealing with the operations of the organization. Operational managers may provide input into the formulation of strategic plans, but such plans are formulated by the planning group. Operational managers are key actors in implementing components of strategic plans.

Opponent Person who ran against others in an election for an office or position.

Opportunity Cost Cost of not taking a particular course of action. For example, if there are two issues and one is deemed to be strategic and the other is not, then the opportunity cost is the cost of not pursuing the course of action required for the nonstrategic issue. If the purchase of computers is a strategic issue, and the cost to purchase typewriters is not, then the cost of not acquiring the typewriters is an opportunity cost.

Override To nullify; to pass over.

Pardon To forgive a person for something he/she did wrong; to release or free a person from punishment.

Petition A formal request, usually written, for a right or benefit from a person or group with authority.

Philosophy The general beliefs, attitudes and ideas or theories of a person or group.

Platform The stated principles of a candidate for public office or a political party.

Policy Chosen course of action designed to significantly affect the organization's behavior in prescribed situations.

Political Action Committee (PAC) A group organized to promote its members' views on selected issues, usually through raising money that is contributed to the campaign funds of candidates who support the group's position.

President The Chief Executive Officer of the federal government organization.

Productivity Measure of performance that includes the requirements of both efficiency and effectiveness. Includes performing the program or work tasks correctly (effectively) and economically (efficiently).

Pro Tempore For the time being; temporarily.

Preliminary Introductory; something that comes before and is necessary to what follows.

Preside To hold the position of authority; to be in charge of a meeting or group.

Primary Election Election by which the candidate who will represent a particular political party is chosen.

Ratification Two uses of this term are: (1) the act of approval of a proposed constitutional amendment by the legislatures of the States; (2) the Senate process of advice and consent to treaties negotiated by the President.

Ratify To approve or confirm formally; to make valid and binding.

Redistricting The process within the States of redrawing legislative district boundaries to reflect population changes following the decennial census.

Regional Government A multi-jurisdictional agency that includes any combination of cities and counties, and is usually sub-state in nature. Only a few regional governments involve more than one state.

Regulation Rule or order which controls actions and procedures.

Repeal To take back or recall, usually a law.

Representative Democracy The people choose or elect officials to make decisions for them about their government. On some issues, however, the people vote, rather than their representatives.

Republican Democratic; representative.

Resolution A legislative act without the force of law, such as action taken to adopt a policy or to modify an existing program.

Ruling The official decision of a court on the case being tried.

Sentence Judgment or decision; usually a decision on the punishment for a person convicted of a crime.

Special Purpose Local Governments Includes special districts, which perform a single public service or function (e.g., water, sewer, and transportation districts, to name a few).

Staff Personnel in those departments designed to serve the operating components, or line departments, of an organization (e.g., personnel, finance, general services, purchasing, etc.).

Stakeholder Those individuals, groups, and outside parties that either affect or who are affected by the organization. Examples include constituents, special-interest groups, suppliers, unions, employees, policy-makers, and advisory bodies, to name a few. In any strategic planning process these entities must either be involved or consulted so that their views are given consideration during the planning process.

Strategic Issues Issues included in a strategic plan which are deemed important to the organization and its future performance. These issues may be either internal or external to the organization itself. Typically, external issues are more difficult to manage than internal issues, due to the limited degree of control exercised by public organizations over their outside environment.

Strategic Management Involves setting direction for the organization and typically performed by elected and appointed officials, or some combination of these individuals, once a strategic plan is approved for implementation. While the strategic plan is approved by elected officials, top management is responsible for its administrative implementation.

Strategic Vision Explicit, shared understanding of the nature and purpose of the organization. It specifies what the organization is and should be rather than what it does operationally. The strategic vision is contained within an organization's strategy statement.

Strategy General direction set for the organization and its various components to achieve a desired state in the future. Strategy results from the detailed planning process that assesses the external and internal environment of an organization and results in a work plan that includes mission statements to direct the goals and objectives of the organization.

Structure Segmentation of work into components, typically organized around those goods and services produced, the formal lines of authority and communication between these components, and the information that flows between these communication and authority relationships.

Succession Order in which one person follows another in replacing a person in an office or position.

Table To postpone or delay making a decision on an issue or law.

Time Horizon A timespan included in a plan, or planning document, varies depending on the type of plan being developed. Strategic plans typically have a five or ten year, sometimes longer, time horizon. Operational plans, on the other hand, frequently project a three to five-year timespan into the future.

Unconstitutional In conflict with a constitution.

Veto Power of the head of the executive branch to keep a bill from becoming law.

Editor's Note: Some of the above terms were taken from *U.S. Government Structure* (1987), and *Our American Government* (1993), U.S. Government Printing Office, Washington, D.C. copies of these books may be obtained from the U.S. Government Printing Office, P.O. Box 371954, Pittsburgh, Pennsylvania 15250-7954, or may be ordered over the internet from GPO's online bookstore (http://bookstore.gpo.gov).

B. Local Government Historical Document

(Mecklenburg County was the first local government in America to declare its Independence from Great Britain)

The Mecklenburg Resolution
(May 20, 1775)

I. *Resolved*: That whosoever directly or indirectly abets, or in any way, form, or manner countenances the unchartered and dangerous invasion of our rights, as claimed by Great Britain, is an enemy to this country–to America–and to the inherent and inalienable rights of man.

II. *Resolved*: That we do hereby declare ourselves a free and independent people; are, and of right ought to be a sovereign and self-governing association, under the control of no power, other than that of our God and the General Government of the Congress: To the maintenance of which Independence was solemnly pledge to each other our mutual co-operation, our Lives, our Fortunes, and our most Sacred Honor.

III. *Resolved*: That as we acknowledge the existence and control of no law or legal officer, civil or military, within this county, we do hereby ordain and adopt as a rule of life, all, each, and every one of our former laws, wherein, nevertheless, the Crown of Great Britain never can be considered as holding rights, privileges, or authorities therein.

IV. *Resolved*: That all, each, and every Military Officer in this country is hereby reinstated in his former command and authority, he acting to their regulations, and that every Member present of this Delegation, shall henceforth be a Civil Officer, viz: a Justice of the Peace, in the character of a Committee Man, to issue process, hear and determine all matters of controversy, according to said adopted laws, and to preserve Peace, Union, and Harmony in said county, to use every exertion to spread the Love of Country and Fire of Freedom throughout America, until a more general and organized government be established in this Province

ABRAHAM ALEXANDER, *chairman*.
JOHN MCKNITT ALEXANDER, *Secretary*

REFERENCE

1   This declaration of independence (with supplementary set of resolutions establishing a form of government) was adopted (as it is claimed) by a convention of delegates from different sections of Mecklenburg County, which assembled at Charlotte May 20, 1775.

C. United States Voting Rights History

(Year, Legislation, Impact)

1776	*Declaration of Independence*	Right to vote during the colonial and Revolutionary periods is restricted to property owners.
1787	*United States Constitution*	States are given the power to regulate their own voting rights.
1856	*State Legislation*	North Carolina is the last state to remove property ownership as a requirement for voting.
1868	*14th Amendment to the U.S. Constitution*	Citizenship is granted to all former slaves. Voters are still defined as male. Voting regulations are still a right of the states.
1870	*15th Amendment to the U.S. Constitution*	It is now law that the right to vote cannot be denied by the federal or state governments based on race.
1887	*Daws Act*	Citizenship is granted to Native Americans who give up their Tribal affiliations.
1890	*State Constitution*	Wyoming is admitted to statehood and becomes the first state to Legislate voting rights for women in its state constitution.
1913	*17th Amendment to the U.S. Constitution*	New law that allows citizens to vote for members of the U.S. Senate, instead of the past practice of having them elected by State Legislatures.
1915	*U.S. Supreme Court Decision*	The U.S. Supreme Court outlawed, in *Guinn v. United States* (Oklahoma), literacy tests for federal elections. The court Ruled that this practice was in violation of the 15th Amendment To the U.S. Constitution.
1920	*19th Amendment to the U.S. Constitution*	Women were given the right to vote in both state and federal elections.
1924	*Indian Citizenship*	This law granted all Native Americans the rights of citizenship, Including the right to vote in federal elections.

1944	*U.S. Supreme Court Decision*	The U.S. Supreme Court outlawed in *Smith v. Allright* (Texas), "white primaries" in Texas and other States. The court ruled that this practice was in violation of the 15th Amendment to the U.S. Constitution.
1957	*Civil Rights Act*	The first law to implement the 15th Amendment to the U.S. Constitution is passed. This law established the Civil Rights Commission, which formally investigates complaints of voter Discrimination made by citizens.
1960	*U.S. Supreme Court Decision*	The U.S. Supreme Court, in *Gomillion v. Lightfoot* (Alabama), outlawed the use of "gerrymandering" in election practices. This practice includes boundary determination (or Redistricting) changes being made for electoral advantage.
1961	*23rd Amendment to the U.S. Constitution*	Citizens of Washington, DC, are given the right to vote in presidential elections.
1964	*24th Amendment to the U.S. Constitution*	The right for citizens to vote in federal elections cannot be denied for failure to pay a poll tax.
1965	*Voting Rights Act*	This law forbids states from imposing discriminatory restrictions on the voting rights of citizens, and provides mechanisms to the federal government for the enforcement of this law. This Act was expanded and renewed in 1970, 1975, 1982, and 2006.
1966	*U.S. Supreme Court Decision*	The U.S. Supreme Court, in *Harper v. Virginia Board of Education* (Virginia), eliminated the poll tax as qualification for voting in any election. This practice was found to be in Violation of the 24th Amendment to the U.S. Constitution.
1966	*U.S. Supreme Court Decision*	The U.S Supreme Court, in *South Carolina v. Katzenbach* (South Carolina), upheld the legality of the Voting Rights Act of 1965.
1970	*U.S. Supreme Court Decision*	The U.S. Supreme Court, in *Oregon v. Mitchell* (Oregon), upheld the ban on the use of literacy tests as a requirement for voting. This ban was made permanent in the 1975 Amendment to the Voting Rights Act.
1971	*26th Amendment to the U.S. Constitution*	The national legal voting age is reduced from 21 years old to 18 years old.

1972	*U.S. Supreme Court Decision*	The U.S. Supreme Court, in *Dunn v. Blumstein* (Tennessee), ruled that lengthy residency requirements for voting in state and local elections are unconstitutional, and suggested a 30-day Residency period as being adequate.
1975	*Amendments to the Voting Rights Act*	Mandated that certain voting materials must be printed in languages besides English so that people who do not read English can participate in the voting process.
1993	*National Voter Registration Act*	Attempts to increase the number of eligible citizens who register to vote by making registration available at each state's Department of Motor Vehicles, as well as public assistance and disability agencies.
2002	*Help America Vote Act*	Law requires that states comply with federal mandates for Provisional ballots; disability access; centralized, computerized voting lists; electronic voting; and the requirement that first-time voters present identification before they can vote.
2003	*Federal Voting Standards And Procedures Act*	Requires all states to streamline their voter registration process, voting practices, and election procedures.

NOTE

For additional information concerning these documents, and related information, please refer to the *Federal Election Commission*, which is listed in the *National Resource Directory* section of this volume.

D. National Resource Directory

(organized by topics for the public, nonprofit, and educational sectors)

Civic Education

Ackerman Center for Democratic Citizenship
(http://www.education.purdue.edu/ackerman-center)

American Democracy Project
(http://www.aascu.org/programs/adp/)

Bill of Rights Institute
(http://www.civiced.org/)

Center for Civic Education
(http://www.civiced.org/)

Center for Youth Citizenship
(http://www.youthcitizenship.org/)

Civic Education Project
(http://www.civiceducationproject.org/)

Civnet
(http://civnet.org/)

Constitutional Rights Foundation
(http://www.crf-usa.org/)

Kellogg Foundation
(http://www.wkkf.org/)

Civic Renewal Initiative
(http://www.ncoc.org/)

National Endowment for Democracy
(http://www.ned.org/)

National Institute for Citizens Education and Law
(https://eric.ed.gov)

Civil Rights and Civil Liberties

American Civil Liberties Union
(http://www.aclu.org/)

Citizens Commission on Civil Rights
(http://www.cccr.org/)

Constitution Society
(http://www.constitution.org/)

Freedom Forum
(http://www.freedomforum.org/)

Judicial Watch
(http://www.judicialwatch.org/)

League of Women Voters
(http://www.lwv.org/)

National Coalition again Censorship
(http://www.ncac.org/)

Project Vote Smart
(http://www.vote-smart.org/)

Historical

Center for the Study of Federalism
(http://www.federalism.org/)

Center for the Study of the Presidency
(http://www.thepresidency.org/)

Constitutional Facts
(http://www.constitutionfacts.com/)

Freedom Foundation at Valley Forge
(http://www.ffvf.org/)

National Constitution Center
(http://www.constitutioncenter.org/)

Supreme Court Historical Society
(http://www.supremecourthistory.org/)

The Avalon Project
(http://www.law.yale.edu/)

White House Historical Association
(http://www.whitehousehistory.org/)

Political Parties

Democratic National Committee
(http://www.democrats.org/)

Green Party of North America
(http://www.greens.org/)

Libertarian Party
(http://www.lp.org/)

Natural Law Party
(http://www.natural-law.org/)

Reform Party
(http://www.reformparty.org/)

Republican National Committee
(http://www.gop.com/)

Socialist Party
(http://www.socialist.org/)

Professional Associations

American Bar Association
(http://www.abanet.org/)

American Planning Association
(http://www.planning.org/)

American Political Science Association
(http://www.apsanet.org/)

American Society for Public Administration
(http://www.aspanet.org/)

Association for Metropolitan Planning Organizations
(http://www.ampo.org/)

Public Policy

Association for Public Policy Analysis and Management
(http://www.appam.org/)

Center for Policy Alternatives
(http://www.cfpa.org/)

Center for Public Integrity
(http://www.publicintegrity.org/)

Common Cause
(http://www.commoncause.org/)

National Center for Policy Analysis
(http://www.ncpa.org/)

National Center for Public Policy Research
(http://www.nationalcenter.org/)

National Legal Center for Public Interest
(http://www.nlcpi.org/)

Pew Research Center
(http://pewresearch.org/)

State and Local Government

Council of State Governments
(http://www.csg.org/)

International City/Country Management Association
(http://www.icma.org/)

Local Government Commission
(http://www.lgc.org/)

Meyner Center for the study of State and Local Government
(https://meynercenter.lafayette.edu/)

National Association of Counties
(http://www.naco.org/)

National Association of Regional Councils
(http://www.narc.org/)

National Association of Towns and Townships
(http://natat.org/)

National Center for State Courts
(http://www.ncsc.org/)

National Civic League
(http://www.ncl.org/)

National Conference of State Legislatures
(http://www.ncsl.org/)

National Governors Association
(http://www.nga.org/)

National League of Cities
(http://www.nlc.org/)

Secretary of State/State of Connecticut
(http://www.sots.ct.gov/)

U.S. Conference of Mayors
(http://www.usmayors.org/)

State Supreme Judicial Court Commonwealth of Massachusetts
(http://www.mass.gov/courts/sjcl/)

U.S. Government

Federal Communications Commission
(http://www.fcc.gov/)

Federal Elections Commission
(http://www.fec.gov/)

Federal Judicial Center
(http://www.fjc.gov/)

Federal Judiciary Homepage
(http://www.uscourts.gov/)

Library of Congress
(http://lcweb.loc.gov/)

National Endowment for the Humanities
(http://www.neh.gov/)

Thomas Legislative Information
(http://www.congress.gov/)

U.S. Census Bureau
(http://www.census.gov/)

U.S. Department of State
(http://www.state.gov/)

U.S. Department of the Interior
(http://www.doi.gov/)

U.S. House of Representatives
(http://www.house.gov/)

U.S. National Archives and Records Administration
(http://www.archives.gov/)

U.S. Senate
(http://www.senate.gov/)

U.S. Supreme Court
(http://www.supremecourtus.gov/)

White House
(http://www.whitehouse.gov/)

Others

Brookings Institution
(http://www.Brookings.edu/)

Civics & The Future of Democracy
(http://futureofcivics.theatlantic.com)

Heritage Foundation
(http://www.heritage.org/)

National Humanities Institute
(http://www.nhinet.org/)

National Taxpayers Union
(http://www.ntu.org/)

National Urban League
(http://www.nul.org/)

Smithsonian Institution
(http://www.si.edu/)

Street Law, Inc.
(http://www.streetlaw.org/)

Supreme Court Decisions
(http://supct.law.cornell.edu/supct/)

United Kingdom Parliamentary Archives
(http://www.parliament.uk/archives/)

Urban Institute
(http://www.urban.org/)

Wikipedia Encyclopedia
(http://www.wikipedia.org/)

NOTE

Some professional association are listed under headings that fit their primary mission. Those that don't fit into one of the general topics are listed under "others."

E. State Municipal League Directory

Most states have a municipal league, which serves as a valuable source of information about city government innovations and programs. Additional information on eminent domain is available from the following state municipal league websites:

Alabama League of Municipalities
(http://www.alalm.org/)

Alaska Municipal League
(http://www.akml.org/)

League of Arizona Cities and Towns
(http://www.azleague.org/)

Arkansas Municipal League
(http://www.arml.org/)

League of California Cities
(http://www.cacities.org/)

Colorado Municipal League
(http://www.cml.org/)

Connecticut Conference of Municipalities
(http://www.ccm-ct.org/)

Delaware League of Local Governments
(http://www.ipa.udel.edu/localgovt/dllg/)

Florida League of Cities
(http://www.flcities.com/)

Georgia Municipal Association
(http://www.gmanet.com/)

Association of Idaho Cities
(http://www.idahocities.org/)

Illinois Municipal League
(http://www.iml.org/)

Indiana Association of Cities and Towns
(http://www.citiesandtowns.org/)

Iowa League of Cities
(http://www.iowaleague.org/)

League of Kansas Municipalities
(http://www.lkm.org/)

Kentucky League of Cities, Inc.
(http://www.klc.org/)

Louisiana Municipal Association
(http://www.lma.org/)

Maine Municipal Association
(http://www.memun.org/)

Maryland Municipal League
(http://www.mdmunicipal.org/)

Massachusetts Municipal Association
(http://www.mma.org/)

Michigan Municipal League
(http://www.mml.org/)

League of Minnesota Cities
(http://www.lmc.org/)

Mississippi Municipal League
(http://www.mmlonline.com/)

Missouri Municipal League
(http://www.mocities.com/)

Montana League of Cities and Towns
(http://www.mtleague.org/)

League of Nebraska Municipalities
(http://www.lonm.org/)

Nevada League of Cities and Municipalities
(http://www.nvleague.org/)

New Hampshire Municipal Association
(http://www.nhmunicipal.org/)

New Jersey State League of Municipalities
(http://www.njlm.org/)

New Mexico Municipal League
(http://nmml.org/)

New York State Conference of Mayors and Municipal Officials
(http://www.nycom.org/)

North Carolina League of Municipalities
(http://www.nclm.org/)

North Dakota League of Cities
(http://www.ndlc.org/)

Ohio Municipal League
(http://www.omlohio.org/)

Oklahoma Municipal League
(http://www.oml.org/)

League of Oregon Cities
(http://www.orcities.org/)

Pennsylvania Municipal League
(http://www.pml.org/)

Rhode Island League of Cities And Towns
(http://www.rileague.org/)

Municipal Association of South Carolina
(http://www.masc.sc/)

South Dakota Municipal League
(http://www.sdmunicpalleague.org/)

Tennessee Municipal League
(http://www.tmll.org/)

Texas Municipal League
(http://www.tml.org/)

Utah League of Cities and Towns
(http://www.ulct.org/)

Vermont League of Cities and Towns
(http://www.vlct.org/)

Virginia Municipal League
(http://www.vml.org/)

Association of Washington Cities
(http://www.awcnet.org/)

West Virginia Municipal League
(http://www.wvml.org/)

League of Wisconsin Municipalities
(http://www.lwm-info.org/)

Wyoming Association of Municipalities
(http://www.wyomuni.org/)

F. State Library Directory

Most state libraries have copies of state laws, both proposed and adopted in an on-line database. Many states also have copies of the various laws adopted in those cities and towns within their jurisdictions. They are an excellent resource for eminent domain.

Alabama
Alabama Department of Archives & History,
(http://archives.state.al.us/)

Alabama Public Library Services
(http://statelibrary.alabama.gov/)

Alaska
Alaska State Library
(http://www.library.alaska.gov/)

Arizona
Arizona Department of Library, Archives and Public Records
(http://www.azlibrary.gov/)

Arkansas
Arkansas State Library
(http://www.asl.lib.ar.us/)

California
California State Library
(http://www.library.ca.gov/)

Colorado
Colorado State Library and Adult Education Office
(http://www.cde.state.co.us/cdelib/)

Colorado Virtual Library
(http://www.coloradovirtuallibrary.org/)

Connecticut
Connecticut State Library
(http://www.ctstatelibrary.org/)

Delaware

Delaware Library Catalog Consortium
(https://lib.de.us/about-us/about-dlc/)

Delaware Division of Libraries
(http://www.libraries.delaware.gov/)

District of Columbia

District of Columbia Public Library
(http://www.dclibrary.org/)

Florida

State Library and Archives of Florida
(http://www.dos.myflorida.com/library-archive/)

Georgia

Office of Public Library Services
(http://www.georgialibraries.org/)

Hawaii

Hawaii State Public Library System
(http://www.librarieshawaii.org/)

Idaho

Idaho Commission for Libraries
(http://libraries.idaho.gov/)

Illinois

Illinois State Library
(http://www.cyberdriveillinois.com/department/library)

Indiana

Indiana State Library
(http://www.in.gov/library/)

Iowa

State Library of Iowa
(http://www.statelibraryofiowa.org/)

Kansas

Kansas State Library
(http://www.kslib.info/)

Kentucky
Kentucky Department for Libraries and Archives
(http://www.kdla.ky.gov/)

Louisiana
State Library of Louisiana
(http://www.state.lib.la.us/)

Maine
Maine State Library
(http://www.state.me.us/msl.)

Maryland
Sailor: Maryland's Public Information Network
(http://www.sailor.lib.md.us/)

Massachusetts
Massachusetts Board of Library Commissioners
(http://mblc.state.ma.us/)

Michigan
Library of Michigan
(http://www.michigan.gov/libraryofmichigan)

Minnesota
State Government Libraries
(http://www.libraries.state.mn.us/)

Mississippi
Mississippi Library Commission
(http://www.mlc.lib.ms.us/)

Missouri
Missouri State Library
(http://www.sos.mo.gov/library/)

Montana
Montana State Library
(http://www.home.msl.mt.gov/)

Nebraska
Nebraska Library Commission
(http://www.nlc.state.ne.us/)

Nevada
Nevada State Library and Archives
(http://www.nsladigitalcollections.org)

New Hampshire
New Hampshire State Library
(http://www.nh.gov/nhsl/)

New Jersey
The New Jersey State Library
(http://www.njstatelib.org/)

New Mexico
New Mexico State Library
(http://www.nmstatelibrary.org/)

New York
The New York State Library
(http://www.nysl.nysed.gov/)

New York State Archives
(http://www.archives.nysed.gov/)

North Carolina
State Library of North Carolina
(https://statelibrary.ncdcr.gov/)

North Dakota
North Dakota State Library
(http://www.library.nd.gov/)

Ohio
State Library of Ohio
(http://www.library.ohio.gov/)

Oklahoma
Oklahoma Department of Libraries
(http://www.odl.state.ok.us/)

Oregon
Oregon State Library
(http://oregon.gov/OSL/)

Pennsylvania
State Library of Pennsylvania
(https://www.statelibrary.pa.gov/)

Rhode Island
Office of Library and Information Services
(http://www.olis.ri.gov/)

South Carolina
South Carolina State Library
(http://www.statelibrary.sc.gov/)

South Dakota
South Dakota State Library
(http://library.sd.gov/)

Tennessee
Tennessee State Library & Archives
(http://www.tennessee.gov/tsla/)

Texas
Texas State Library and Archives Commission
(http://www.tsl.state.tx.us/)

Utah
Utah State Library
(http://library.utah.gov/)

Vermont
Vermont Department of Libraries
(http://libraries.vermont.gov/)

Virginia
The Library of Virginia
(http://www.lva.virginia.gov/)

Washington
Washington State Library
(http://www.secstate.wa.gov/library/)

West Virginia
West Virginia Library Commission
(http://wvlc.lib.wv.us/)

West Virginia Archives and History
(http://www.wvculture.org/history/)

Wisconsin

Wisconsin Department of Public Instruction: Division for Libraries, Technology, and Community Learning
(http://www.dpi.wi.gov/dltcl/)

Wyoming

Wyoming State Library
(http://www.library.wyo.gov/)

G. Books by Roger L. Kemp

(as author, contributing author, and editor)

(1) Roger L Kemp, ***Coping with Proposition 13***, Lexington Books, D.C. Heath and Company, Lexington, MA, and Toronto, Canada (1980)

(2) Roger L. Kemp, "The Administration of Scarcity: Managing Government in Hard Times," ***Conferencia De Las Grandes Ciudades De Las America***, Interamerican Foundation of Cities, San Juan, Puerto Rico (1983)

(3) Roger L. Kemp**, *Cutback Management: A trinational Perspective***, Transaction Books, New Brunswick, NJ, and London, England (1983)

(4) Roger L. Kemp, ***Research in Urban Policy: Coping with Urban Austerity***, JAI Press, Inc., Greenwich, CT, and London, England (1985)

(5) Roger L. Kemp, ***America's Infrastructure: Problems and Prospects***, The Interstate Printers and Publishers, Danville, IL (1986)

(6) Roger L. Kemp, ***Coping with Proposition 13: Strategies for Hard Times***, Robert E. Krieger Publishing Company, Malabar, FL (1988)

(7) Roger L Kemp, ***America's Cities: Strategic Planning for the Future***, The Interstate Printers and Publishers, Danville, IL (1988)

(8) Roger L. Kemp, ***The Hidden Wealth of Cities: Policy and Productivity Methods for American Local Governments***, JAI Press, Inc., Greenwich, CT and London, England (1989)

(9) Roger L. Kemp, ***Strategic Planning in Local Government: A Casebook***, Planners Press, American Planning Association, Chicago, IL, and Washington, D.C. (1992)

(10) Roger L. Kemp, ***Strategic Planning for Local Government***, International City/County Management Association, Washington, D.C. (1993)

(11) Roger L. Kemp, ***America's Cities: Problems and Prospects***, Avebury Press, Alershot, England (1995)

(12) Roger L. Kemp, ***Helping Business - The Library's Role in Community Economic Development, A How-To-D-It Manual***, Neal-Schuman Publishers, Inc., New York, NY, and London, England (1997)

(13) Roger L. Kemp, ***Homeland Security: Best Practices for Local Government***, 1st Edition, International City/County Management Association, Washington, D.C. (2003)

(14) Roger L Kemp, ***Cities and the Arts: A handbook for Renewal***, McFarland & Company, Inc., Jefferson, NC (2004)

(15) Roger L. Kemp, ***Homeland Security Handbook for Citizen and Public Officials***, McFarland & Company, Inc., Jefferson, NC (2006)

(16) Roger L. Kemp, ***Main Street Renewal: A Handbook for Citizens and Public Officials***, McFarland & Company, Inc., Jefferson, NC (2006, 2000)

(17) Roger L. Kemp, *Local Government Election Practices: A Handbook for Public Officials and Citizens*, McFarland & Company, Inc., Jefferson, NC (2006, 1999)

(18) Roger L. Kemp, *Cities and Nature: A Handbook for Renewal*, McFarland & Company, Inc., Jefferson, NC (2006)

(19) Roger L. Kemp, *Emergency Management and Homeland Security*, International City/County Management Association, Washington, D.C. (2006)

(20) Roger L. Kemp, *The Inner City: A Handbook for Renewal*, McFarland & Company, Inc., Jefferson, NC (2007, 2001)

(21) Roger L. Kemp, *Privatization: The Provision of Public Services by the Private Sector*, McFarland & Company, Inc., Jefferson, NC (2007, 1991)

(22) Roger L. Kemp, *Community Renewal through Municipal Investment: A Handbook for Citizens and Public Officials*, McFarland & Company, Inc., Jefferson, NC (2007, 2003)

(23) Roger L. Kemp, *How American Government Works: A Handbook on City, County, Regional, State, and Federal Operations*, McFarland & Company, Inc., Jefferson, NC (2007, 2002)

(24) Roger L. Kemp, *Regional Government Innovations: A Handbook for Citizens and Public Officials*, McFarland & Company, Inc., Jefferson, NC (2007, 2003)

(25) Roger L. Kemp, *Economic Development in Local Government: A Handbook for Public Officials and Citizens*, McFarland & Company, Inc.., Jefferson, NC (2007, 1995)

(26) Roger L. Kemp, *Model Practices for Municipal Governments*, Connecticut Town and City Management Association, University of Connecticut, West Hartford, CT (2007)

(27) Roger L. Kemp, *Managing America's Cities: A Handbook for Local Government Productivity*, McFarland & Company, Inc., Jefferson, NC (2007, 1998)

(28) Roger L. Kemp, *Model Government Charters: A City, County, Regional, State, and Federal Handbook*, McFarland & Company, Inc., Jefferson, NC (2007, 2003)

(29) Roger L. Kemp, *Forms of Local Government: A Handbook on City, County and Regional Options*, McFarland & Company, Inc., Jefferson, NC (2007, 1999)

(30) Roger L. Kemp, *Cities and Cars: A Handbook of Best Practices*, McFarland & Company, Inc., Jefferson, NC (2007)

(31) Roger L. Kemp, *Homeland Security for the Private Sector: A Handbook*, McFarland & Company, Inc., Jefferson, NC (2007)

(32) Roger L. Kemp, *Strategic Planning for Local Government: A Handbook for Officials and Citizens*, McFarland & Company, Inc., Jefferson, NC (2008, 1993)

(33) Roger L. Kemp, *Museums, Libraries and Urban Vitality: A Handbook*, McFarland & Company, Inc., Jefferson, NC (2008)

(34) Roger L. Kemp, *Cities and Growth: A Policy Handbook*, McFarland & Company, Inc., Jefferson, NC (2008)

(35) Roger L. Kemp, *Cities and Sports Stadiums: A Planning Handbook*, McFarland & Company, Inc., Jefferson, NC (2009)

(36) Roger L. Kemp, *Cities and Water: A Handbook for Planning*, McFarland & Company, Inc., Jefferson, NC (2009)

(37) Roger L. Kemp, *Homeland Security: Best Practices for Local Government*, 2nd Edition, International city/County Management Association, Washington, D.C. (2010)

(38) Roger L. Kemp, *Cities and Adult Businesses: A Handbook for Regulatory Planning*, McFarland & Company, Inc., Jefferson, NC (2010)

(39) Roger L. Kemp, *Documents of American Democracy: A Collection of Essential Works*, McFarland & Company, Inc., Jefferson, NC (2010)

(40) Roger L. Kemp, *Strategies and Technologies for a Sustainable Future*, World Future Society, Bethesda, MD (2010)

(41) Roger L. Kemp, *Cities Going Green: A Handbook of Best Practices*, McFarland & Company, Inc., Jefferson, NC (2011)

(42) Roger L. Kemp, *The Municipal Budget Crunch: A Handbook for Professionals*, McFarland & Company, Inc., Jefferson, NC (2012)

(43) Roger L. Kemp, Frank B. Connolly, and Philip K. Schenck, *Local Government in Connecticut*, 3rd Edition, Wesleyan University Press, Middletown, CT (2013)

(44) Roger L. Kemp, *Town and Gown Relations: A Handbook of Best Practices*, McFarland & Company, Inc., Jefferson, NC (2013)

(45) Roger L. Kemp, *Global Models of Urban Planning: Best Practices Outside the United States*, McFarland & Company, Inc., Jefferson, NC (2013)

(46) Roger L. Kemp, *Urban Transportation Innovations Worldwide: A Handbook of Best Practices Outside the United States*, McFarland & Company, Inc., Jefferson, NC (2015)

(47) Roger L. Kemp, *Immigration and America's Cities: A Handbook on Evolving Services*, McFarland & Company, Inc., Jefferson, NC (2016)

(48) Roger L. Kemp, *Corruption and American Cities: Essays and Case Studies in Ethical Accountability*, McFarland & Company, Jefferson, NC (2016)

(49) Roger L. Kemp, *Privatization in Practice: Reports on Trends, Cases and Debates in Public Service by Business and Nonprofits*, McFarland & Company, Inc., Jefferson, NC (2016)

(50) Roger L. Kemp, *Small Town Economic Development: Reports on Growth Strategies in Practice*, McFarland & Company, Inc., Jefferson, NC (2017)

(51) Roger L. Kemp, Donald F. Norris, Laura Mateczun, Cory Fleming, and Will Fricke, *Cybersecurity: Protecting Local Government Digital Resources*, International City/County Management Association, Washington, D.C. (2017)

(52) Roger L. Kemp, *Eminent Domain and Economic Growth: Perspectives on Benefits, Harms and Trends*, McFarland & Company, Inc., Jefferson, NC (2018)

(53) Roger L. Kemp, *Senior Care and Services: Essays and Case Studies on Practices, Innovations and Challenges*, McFarland & Company, Inc., Jefferson, NC (2019)

(54) Roger L. Kemp, *Cybersecurity: Current Writings on Threats and Protection*, McFarland & Company, Inc., Jefferson, NC (2019)

(55) Roger L. Kemp, *Veteran Care and Services: Essays and Case Studies on Practices, Innovations and Challenges*, McFarland & Company, Inc., Jefferson, NC (2020)

(56) Roger L. Kemp, *Civics 101 – Poems About America's Cities*, Kindle Direct Publishing, Middletown, DE (2020)

(57) Roger L. Kemp, *Civics 102 – Stories About America's Cities*, Kindle Direct Publishing, Middletown, DE (2121)

(58) Roger L. Kemp, *Civics 103 – Charters that Form America's Governments*, Kindle Direct Publishing, Middletown, DE (2121)

(59) Roger L. Kemp, *Civics 104 – America's Evolving Boundaries*, Kindle Direct Publishing, Middletown, DE (2121)

(60) Roger L. Kemp, *Civics 105 – Documents that Formed America*, Kindle Direct Publishing, Middletown, DE (2021)

(61) Roger L. Kemp, *Civics 106 – Documents that Formed the United Kingdom and the United States*, Kindle Direct Publishing, Middletown, DE (2021)

H. World Travels by Roge L. Kemp

Roger has visited the following countries, and major geographic regions, throughout the world during his public service and consulting career:

- Australia*
- Austria
- Belgium
- Brunei Darussalam
- Canada
- China
- Czech Republic
- Fiji
- France*
- French Polynesia*
- Germany*
- Hong Kong*
- Hungary
- Iceland
- Indonesia*
- Italy*
- Japan*
- Luxembourg*
- Macau
- Malaysia*
- Mexico
- Netherlands
- New Zealand*
- Philippines*
- Puerto Rico*
- Singapore*
- Slovak Republic
- South Korea*
- Switzerland
- Tahiti*
- Thailand
- United Kingdom*
- United States (all regions, and most states)*
- Virgin Islands

*During his visits to many of these locations. Dr. Kemp has met with elected officials, such as a city's Mayor, administrative officers, and department managers. He has also given presentations at several international professional conferences in some of these nations.

I. Some Final Thoughts

Thoughts About America's Cities

El Condor Pasa (If I Could)

I'd rather be a forest than a street.
Yes I would, If I could, I surely would.

I'd rather feel the earth beneath my feet.
Yes I would, If I only could, I surely would.

Simon and Garfunkel, 1970

- - -

America's Livable Cities

Our cities were not designed by city planners,
but by cars, to make the vehicle roadways
and parking spaces available for them.

Out cities must be redesigned by city planners,
to enhance the level of nature within them,
for everyone, especially the citizens who live in our cities.

Roger L. Kemp, 2020

NOTES

1   The January 14, 1638 date was in the old style Julian Calendar, before conversion to the modern new style Gregorian Calendar.

2   "Fundamental Orders." *The Columbia Encyclopedia, Sixth Edition.* Columbia University Press. 2005.

3   Lutz, Donald S.; Schechter, Stephen L.; Bernstein, Richard J. (1990). *Roots of the Republic: American founding documents interpreted.* Madison, Wis: Madison House. Pp. 24. ISBN 0-945612-19-2.

4   Secretary of the State of Connecticut (2007). "STATE OF CONNECTICUT Sites Seals Symbols. *The Connecticut State Register and Manual.* State of Connecticut.

5   Horton, Wesley W. (1993-06-30). *The Connecticut State Constitution: A Reference Guide.* Reference guides to the state constitutions of the United States. No. 17. Westport, Connecticut: Greenwood Press. pp. 2.

6   Taylor, John M. *Roger Ludlow: The Colonial Lawmaker.* G.P. Putnam's Sons, New York, NY, 1990.

7   Primarily the work of Thomas Jefferson and John Dickinson. p. 168 Morison, Samuel Eliot, Henry Steele Commager, and William E. Leuchtenburg. *The Growth of the American Republic: Volume I.* Seventh Edition. New York: Oxford University Press; 1980. (Note added by the Avalon Project).

8   From this point the declaration follows Jefferson's draft.

9   Preamble, Virginia Declaration of Rights.

10   Lieberman, Jethro (1987). *The Enduring Constitution: A Bicentennial Perspective.* West Publishing Co., p. 28.

11   Mr. Ferdinand Jefferson, Keeper of the Rolls in the Department of State, at Washington, says: "The names of the signers are spelt above as in the facsimile of the original, but the punctuation of them is not always the same; neither do the names of the States appear in the facsimile of the original. The names of the signers of each State are grouped together in the facsimile of the original, except the name of Matthew Thornton, which follows that of Oliver Wolcott." – Revised Statutes of the United States, 2d edition, 1878, p. 6.

12   The first local government in the American colonies to declare its independence from Great Britain was Mecklenburg County, North Carolina, on May 20, 1775. The county declared its independence from Great Britain immediately after the Battle of Lexington, in what is now called the Commonwealth of Massachusetts. Additional information concerning the "Mecklenburg Declaration of Independence" can be found on the Library of Congress website, which is listed in the *National Resource Directory* section of this volume. Because of its significance, this document is shown in its entirety in the Appendix of this volume under the heading "Local Government Historical Document."

INDEX

Printed in the United States
by Baker & Taylor Publisher Services